CAPTURING NUREYEV

JAMES WYETH PAINTS THE DANCER

Introduction by Clive Barnes

Essays by Barbara Cohen-Stratyner and Lauren Raye Smith

With contributions by Phyllis M. Wyeth and Lynn Seymour

Edited by Pamela J. Belanger

Farnsworth Art Museum

Distributed by University Press of New England

CAPTURING: *to preserve in a relatively permanent form; to captivate and hold the interest of.*

Published on the occasion of the exhibition *Capturing Nureyev: James Wyeth Paints the Dancer,* organized by the Farnsworth Art Museum, Rockland, Maine, in collaboration with The John F. Kennedy Center for the Performing Arts, Washington, D.C., and The New York Public Library for the Performing Arts Dorothy and Lewis B. Cullman Center, New York, and sponsored by the MBNA Foundation.

The John F. Kennedy Center for the Performing Arts
Washington, D.C.
February 7–March 10, 2002

The New York Public Library for the Performing Arts Dorothy and Lewis B. Cullman Center
New York
March 22–May 25, 2002

Farnsworth Art Museum
Rockland, Maine
June 9, 2002–January 5, 2003

Brandywine River Museum
Chadds Ford, Pennsylvania
January 18–May 18, 2003

Designed by MBNA America

ISBN 0-918749-10-7 (clothbound)

Distributed through the University Press of New England

Front Cover: James Wyeth; *Full Face and Partial Chest, Head, Nureyev (Study #10);* 1977; (detail, Fig. 35)

Frontispiece: James Wyeth; *Full Face and Partial Chest, Head, Nureyev (Study #10);* 1977; (detail, Fig. 35)

Back Cover: James Wyeth; *Curtain Call;* 2001; (detail, Fig. 69)

Front End Paper: Michael McKenzie; *James Wyeth Measuring Rudolf Nureyev;* 1977; (detail, Fig. 45)
Costume from *Don Quixote,* Act III, Basilio, 1966 Production

Back End Paper: Michael McKenzie; *James Wyeth Measuring Rudolf Nureyev;* 1977; (detail, Fig. 45)
Costume from *Raymonda,* Act III, Jean de Brienne, 1972 Production

Contents

PREFACE AND ACKNOWLEDGMENTS

Christopher B. Crosman, Michael M. Kaiser, and Jacqueline Z. Davis

Visual artists have long been fascinated by dance. Throughout history and in every culture, from the dance of Shiva to Degas, from Minoan frescoes to Matisse, painters and sculptors have attempted to capture the essence of this most elemental and ephemeral form of human expression. Direct collaboration among visual and performing artists is, however, a relatively recent phenomenon dating to the early years of the twentieth century. Pablo Picasso's set designs for the Russian impresario Diaghilev, are, perhaps, the best known instance of the modern notion of the *gesamtkunstwerk*, the attempt on the part of artists, often across disciplines, to create a "total" aesthetic experience—sound, motion, color, and form—most recently manifested in the collaborations between Robert Wilson and Philip Glass or Alex Katz's backdrops for the Paul Taylor Dance Company.

James Wyeth's paintings of Rudolf Nureyev, however, fit into neither traditional depictions of dance nor the grand scale of twentieth-century multimedia stage productions. Nevertheless, these paintings and studies represent a kind of collaboration between two extraordinary artists who created enduring works of art that explore transformation and stasis, illusion and reality, in the context of personal "presence" and theater. First and foremost, this publication tells the story of one artist's attempt to "capture" the body and spirit of another artist through a sustained series of intimate and revealing portraits that individually and collectively go far beyond likeness and move toward essence.

This publication and exhibition are also an unusual collaboration among three very different types of institutions. It is, indeed, the first collaboration among The John F. Kennedy Center for the Performing Arts, The New York Public Library for the Performing Arts Dorothy and Lewis B. Cullman Center, and the Farnsworth Art Museum. A richly contextualized project, *Capturing Nureyev* is the result of the energy and efforts of a large number of people at each institution as well as individuals who assisted behind the scenes in various capacities.

We must acknowledge that this project would not have been possible without the artist, James Wyeth. James's wife Phyllis also developed a warm friendship with the dancer and her personal recollections are touching and insightful—word portraits that accompany selected photographs from her collection. Catherine Stevens and her husband Senator Ted Stevens of Alaska, who serves on the Board of Trustees of the Kennedy Center, first broached the idea of mounting the exhibition at the Kennedy Center to coincide with performances there of the Kirov Ballet at the beginning of a relationship that will bring the Kirov to Washington for the next ten years. Mrs. Stevens has also played a continuing role in bringing all three organizations together and is largely responsible for making the exhibition a reality.

Friends of the three institutions have supported the project in countless ways. We especially thank Mr. Charles Cawley, CEO of MBNA America, whose early, enthusiastic encouragement for this project has been extraordinary. The MBNA Foundation has generously underwritten *Capturing Nureyev,* including the national tour for the exhibition, related programs, and publications. Many others have contributed behind the scenes and we very much appreciate their efforts: Mary Blair, Lady Carla Carlyle, Mary Beth Dolan, Irina Dolgikh, Tessa Kennedy, Heidi Scheing, Dr. Joyce Hill Stoner, Helene Sutton, and Dr. Elizabeth Williamson.

Most of the photographic and documentary materials for the publication and exhibition are from the extensive holdings of the Jerome Robbins Dance Division of The New York Public Library for the Performing Arts. The Library acknowledges the generosity of the Rudolf Nureyev Foundation, the Rudolf Nureyev Dance Foundation, Wallace Potts, Robert Gable, and others for their contributions over the years to The New York Public Library for the Performing Arts's holdings on Nureyev. We appreciate the efforts of the Library staff for developing this part of the exhibition and making these materials available, especially to Madeleine Nichols, Curator of the Jerome Robbins Dance Division, and Conservator Grace Owen. The exhibition was co-curated by Lauren Raye Smith, Assistant Curator and Conservator at the Farnsworth Art Museum, and Barbara Cohen-Stratyner, the Judy R. and Alfred A. Rosenberg Curator of Exhibitions at The New York Public Library for the Performing Arts. Others have generously participated by lending key works of art and related artifacts: Dr. Charles Ansbacher and Ambassador Swanee Hunt; the Brandywine River

Museum, with special thanks to James Duff, Director; Mr. and Mrs. Stephen H. Casey; Philip and Tina DeNormandie; Douce François and Joseph Freitas; Mr. and Mrs. Mark Forgason; Mr. and Mrs. Frank E. Fowler; MBNA America; Albert, Kathlene, and Catharine Parnell; Dr. and Mrs. David A. Skier; Jim and Jocelyn Stewart; Mr. and Mrs. Andrew Wyeth; James and Phyllis M. Wyeth; and others who wish to remain anonymous. We are grateful to everyone for allowing us to share their treasures with our respective audiences in Washington, D.C.; New York City; Rockland, Maine; and Chadds Ford, Pennsylvania.

Richard Molinaroli of MFM Design has designed the exhibition with a sense of visual coherence, excitement, and theater that will also vary at each host institution. The accompanying documentary film by Stephen Labovsky of Full Circle Productions is a sensitive "portrait" of James Wyeth and his friendship with Rudolf Nureyev.

We are most grateful to *New York Post* dance critic Clive Barnes for his precise and elegant introduction to the book, and Lynn Seymour, friend and former colleague of the dancer, who kindly contributed her poignant speech delivered at The New York Public Library in 1999. This publication required a kind of choreography among all three institutions and their staffs who worked closely with consulting designers and editors. Wendy Larsen assisted Phyllis Wyeth with her personal memoirs and exhibition curators Barbara Cohen-Stratyner and Lauren Raye Smith contributed essays exploring the concept of "capturing" the dancer through photography and painting. We thank each of them for their thoughtful and thought-provoking contributions. We are indebted to the design staff at MBNA Advertising for their efforts related to the design and production of this book. Thanks are due Pamela J. Belanger, Curator of Collections at the Farnsworth Museum, for editing and coordinating the overall book production and to Dawn Hall who assisted with proofreading.

We also want to acknowledge with deep appreciation the contributions of photographers whose works appear in the publication: Zoë Dominic; Rick Echlmeyer; Harrison Evans; the estate of Fred Fehl; Caroline Alexander Forgason; Douce

François Freitas, Susan Gray; Janet P. Levitt; Michael McKenzie; Herbert Migdoll; Steve Morrison; Louis Péres; Robin Platzer; Roy Round; Martha Swope; Jack and Linda D. Vartoogian; and Phyllis M. Wyeth.

Administration for the project in all of its varying manifestations was handled by Barbara Cohen-Stratyner at The New York Public Library for the Performing Arts; Roman Terleckyj, Vice-President, Artistic Planning at The Kennedy Center; and at the Farnsworth Museum, Associate Director Victoria Woodhull and Pamela J. Belanger. They deserve special thanks for keeping the entire project on course, on budget, and on an extremely tight schedule.

We believe this exhibition breaks new ground in joining the resources of three arts organizations that view different art forms from somewhat different perspectives, a kind of *leitmotif* of both the exhibition and the publication. From these varying points of view we come together to celebrate our collective appreciation of one artist's view of another, who together captured an extraordinary moment in American culture—a moment fixed in memory at the "still point of the dance."

Christopher B. Crosman
Director
Farnsworth Art Museum

Jacqueline Z. Davis
Barbara G. and Lawrence Fleischman
Executive Director
The New York Public Library
for the Performing Arts Dorothy
and Lewis B. Cullman Center

Michael M. Kaiser
President
The John F. Kennedy Center
for the Performing Arts

Nureyev

Clive Barnes

RUDOLF HAMETOVICH NUREYEV. Born of Tatar parentage on March 17, 1938, on a train as it traveled around Lake Baikal near Irkutsk, a town then in the Soviet Union, quite close to Mongolia. Died on January 6, 1993 in Paris. A dancer. Those are the basic facts, and most even peripherally interested in dance can fill in much of the rest. What can usefully be said without saying too much, or saying too little?

Here are a few career markers, a few reminders and hints, if you like. After a little early training in the Urals town of Ufa, where he was brought up, he arrived at the Kirov School in St. Petersburg in 1955, where his principal teacher, and a major influence on both him and his dancing, was Alexander Pushkin. He joined the Kirov Ballet in 1958. On June 16, 1961 he sensationally defected at Le Bourget Airport in Paris, following the Kirov Ballet's first appearance in the West.

After a year or so of vagabond indecision, Nureyev linked up with Britain's Royal Ballet, forming a partnership with its then reigning ballerina Margot Fonteyn that became one of the legendary ballet pairings of the twentieth century. Soon Nureyev was an international star, and his off-stage partnership with the great Danish dancer Erik Bruhn also exerted a major influence. In 1963 he staged his first ballet, the "Kingdom of the Shades" scene from Petipa's nineteenth-century classic *La Bayadère,* for the Royal Ballet. Although his links with the British company gradually eroded, his work as a ballet *regisseur,* producer, and choreographer expanded throughout the Western world.

As a dancer he was also the first major classical artist to work with modern-dance choreographers and companies, including those of Martha Graham, Paul Taylor, Murray Louis, and José Limón. He appeared in many dance films and also a few features, notably Ken Russell's 1977 movie *Valentino.* From 1983 until 1989 he was artistic director of the Paris Opéra Ballet, and in 1989, when he was fifty-one, he poignantly returned to St. Petersburg to dance in Bournonville's *La Sylphide* with the Kirov Ballet. The last role created for him was in Flemming Flindt's ballet on Thomas Mann's *Death in Venice* in 1991. His last public appearance was as a conductor, conducting a gala performance of Prokofiev's *Romeo and Juliet* for the American Ballet Theatre at the Metropolitan Opera House on May 6, 1992.

Facts, facts, but what kind of dancer was he? Unfortunately, video does neither Nureyev nor Fonteyn complete justice, for they were essentially dancers of presence. Their sheer immediacy was shocking. They took the stage and absorbed it into their personalities—and this theatrical magic no screen can ever capture. Nureyev in particular was a force of nature rather than a realization of art, a fact that Martha Graham herself was quick to realize and appreciate.

It was natural that when he emerged from Russia—in fact it happened before he left St. Petersburg—he would be compared with that earlier legend of twentieth-century dance, Vaslav Nijinsky. Soon after I first met Nureyev, and conducted the first TV interview in English, I felt compelled to ask him the foolish question about Nijinsky, and Nureyev merely smiled wryly and said, "I feel sorry for Nijinsky!"

Yet in a way the comparison almost had to be made. The only person I knew well who had seen both of these legends perform was the revered English dance historian C. W. Beaumont. He certainly confirmed that while in style they had little in common—Nureyev was never particularly successful in roles that had been created for Nijinsky, such as Fokine's *Petrouchka* and *Scheherazade,* or his own *L'Après-midi d'un Faune*—both shared the same animal magnetism and intensity of artistic focus.

Of all the great classic male dancers of the twentieth century—say, along with Nureyev and Nijinsky, whom of course I never saw, Vakhtang Chabukiani, Jean Babilée, and Erik Bruhn—Chabukiani was the most sensational, Babilée the most brilliant, and Bruhn the most perfect. But Nureyev had the power of the possessed and a faculty for possession. He danced with all of himself. Look at the famous video of him in Ali's solo arranged by Chabukiani from *Le Corsaire pas de deux* (a dance which, incidentally, Nureyev introduced in the West) and you will see that technically not all is perfect here. But he dances like a demon, and the kinetic thrust of the solo, even the weight given the steps themselves, are all projected for maximum dramatic effect.

Fonteyn was once asked what it's like to dance with Nureyev in *Giselle,* and she famously replied, "When I look at him I don't see Rudolf, I see Albrecht." The poetic exaggeration of a ballerina trying to exalt a partnership already becoming iconic? Perhaps. Yet, somehow there was a signal truth there, and also a falsehood. Nureyev, when he danced, always became the character— whether it was Albrecht, Romeo, or Henry James's Dr. Sloper in his own ballet version of *Washington Square*—but equally he always elusively remained Nureyev.

This consistency of artistic profile—something noted readily enough in painting or music—this personal signature, is more rare in the performing arts, and rarest of all in dance. But all great dancers have it—see Nureyev, Mikhail Baryshnikov, Andre Eglevsky, Anthony Dowell, Igor Youskevitch, John Gilpin, Peter Martins dance the same role. The steps might be similar, but the tone, a quality beyond technique, will be different.

And Nureyev, that Russian firebird, had inimitable tone. He also exerted, by his example as much as by his productions, an enormous influence on male dancing in the Western world. There is not a boy in any Western dance classroom today who doesn't owe a great deal to Rudolf Nureyev.

I think something of Rudolf's fugitive grace and elusive grandeur is caught in these images by James Wyeth. I remember a time—a New Year's Eve house party if I recall correctly—my wife Trish and I spent with Rudolf and his entourage at the Wyeths' farm when they were working on these portraits. The two artists had an easy rapport and mutual trust. Those qualities emerge from this final result—the evocation of a dancer, to be treasured rather like José Clará's sketches of Isadora Duncan, or Mervyn Peake's evocations of Babilée.

A dancer's life is a short one—a brief explosive flash across a stage darkened by memory. Its preservation and its documentation are enormously precious. Photographs can give something, but perhaps only the painter can reveal the skull beneath the skin, the soul behind the image.

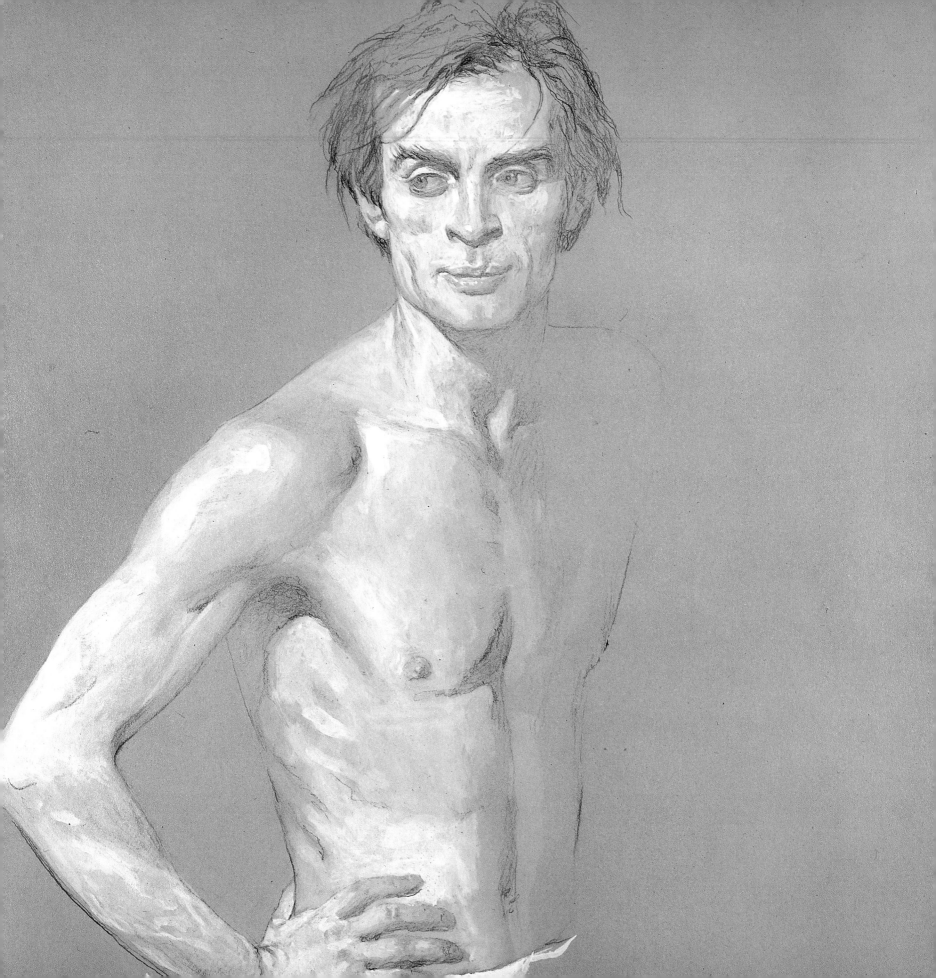

A GREAT MAN

Lynn Seymour

Edited transcript of a speech given October 1999 at The New York Public Library at the announcement of the donation of film, video, television, and sound archives by the Rudolf Nureyev Foundation and the Rudolf Nureyev Dance Foundation to the Jerome Robbins Dance Division, The New York Public Library for the Performing Arts.

In 1998 a small organization in St. Petersburg, Russia, asked a group of Westerners to join them for a symposium to honor Rudolf on what would have been his sixtieth birthday. We went there with a view to describing and discussing the tremendous impact Rudolf has had on the West—the lasting influence and change he had wrought worldwide—how he had inspired three generations of dancers to raise their standards and how he had firmly placed the male dancer on the Western map.

We were extremely surprised to find that the Russians were still suffering from a sense of confusion, grief, and bewilderment at Rudolf's defection and at their continued belief that he had betrayed his school and sold his soul for profit. I was shocked to find that these vehement attitudes and misguided beliefs continued to prevail and that there was no acknowledgment of his years of achievement in the West. I had been so sure that I would find people in Russia who shared my view, that he was a wild Prince destined to become King. Indeed, there were a handful, a minority, who warmly recognized his genius and charisma and who fully understood his thirst to experience the rest of the world.

I attempted to reassure them that Rudolf had never betrayed his school, nor compromised a centimeter of his integrity. In fact, he had waved his schooling like a banner and had educated and elevated every dancer and company he had worked with. Testimony to that was his production of *La Bayadère* for the Royal Ballet in the 1960s, where he imbued a large group of dancers (who had little tradition) into a troupe that was on the road to being able to stand beside the Kirov and Paris Opéra Ballet companies with their centuries of tradition behind them. Of course, we in the West know he never compromised, for we frequently witnessed him refusing to replace a *tour de force* that was eluding him with an easier solution, sometimes with alarming and vertiginous results. This only made us love him more, as we vicariously took part in his derring-do, and experienced the adrenalin rush and that fabulous elation.

Fig. 1 *Half Smile, Nureyev (Study #20);* 1977; Combined Mediums; 20 x 16; Collection of the Artist.

I don't have to convince any of you of his mighty effect on us all, nor do I have to persuade you to recognize the profound influence he had on dance worldwide. Here is a man who was far more than a great dancer. His aura, his charisma, his intelligence, his sheer strength of character caused enormous changes in a remarkably short time. He engaged a hitherto indifferent public in a greater awareness and appreciation of dance in general.

It is no secret that Rudolf's volatility ruffled a lot of feathers and frequently caused offense. But his friends know that this was an essential part of the man and that his provocation stirred lives, and controversy, but most importantly caused action and change. In fact, I see his behavior as another indication of his remarkable courage. Rudolf worshipped at the high altar of his art and was a devoted slave to it. This devotion informed his every action and reaction. If he detected any signs of dishonesty, small mindedness, disregard, crass stupidity, bullshit, or disrespect, if he saw barriers being erected or rules being exercised that would hinder progress, he had to explode. Rudolf detested having his emotions roiled, just as we all do. He detested blowing his top and hated the turmoil and bad atmosphere that would inevitably ensue. But he never compromised his strong beliefs, though it would have been much easier to walk away and save his emotions and energy to better end. Of course, his detractors will never see it that way and will continue to carp. A firm step back from this sort of hubbub is needed in order to see the true thrust of his disconcerting behavior.

On the other side of the coin, when he saw a dancer demonstrating diligence, zeal, intelligence, respect, and devotion to their work he became a warm, generous, and highly supportive mentor who was also a delightful colleague. Rudolf single-handedly kept me buoyant through the greatest troughs and traumas of my career by never wavering in his belief in my talent and regard for my achievements. He was exceptionally tolerant of one's weaknesses and very aware and sensitive to one's hardships. He frequently threw lifelines in times of crisis. They were never big, soft, cozy, inflatable life rafts but rather scary, risky things to grab onto if you dared to. It was often like plunging into the abyss, but you inevitably emerged fortified and with a healthy sense of achievement. Most importantly, you were enabled to continue.

Dancing with Rudolf was the most stimulating thing I have done, and I'm going to try to describe it: During rehearsals he was "teacher extraordinaire," and while not sparing himself in his attempts to improve and consolidate his own performance, he devoted just as much time and energy to helping you do the same. Of course, watching him work and trying to follow his example inspired you to also take risks, recognize bad habits, and find the courage to change them. Time would cease to mean anything until finally, on our last legs, he would announce, "Now let's do it again, not for tomorrow's performance, but for next year." This was the last thing we wanted to do, but by slogging through once more it inevitably paid dividends, for months later, that last painful run-through would come to our aid, when circumstances had allowed for little or no rehearsal. It also alleviated one's fear of fatigue for you had already experienced performing at your lowest ebb.

When it came to the performance, my usually crippling stage fright would be miraculously subdued by the knowledge that Rudolf's courage would infect me and his regard would bolster my self-esteem. Once we were on stage our hard work in the rehearsal room would slip into gear and liberate us to perform. It was heady stuff, risky, dangerous, terrifying, and full of surprises—in fact, a headlong roller coaster ride of unbelievable exhilaration. Quite often we were disappointed with ourselves over some detail, but never with an attitude of defeat. Rather, back to the drawing board. The fantastic rapport that results from going through a performance like this together, time after time, must be akin to those who have experienced and survived together some violent act of nature, or hurtled down the Colorado River. I treasure beyond description the feeling of rapport and those feelings of trust and regard that Rudolf and I shared, for it transcends all other types of relationships and it can never be touched or tarnished by the mundane or the profane.

This experience is not unique to me. Innumerable dancers have been touched by this genius and elevated to loftier heights than they alone were capable of. We are all united in the knowledge that we were blessed by the fates that threw us in his path and that our lives were profoundly enriched through knowing him.

REMEMBERING RUDOLF

Phyllis M. Wyeth with Wendy Larsen

Fig. 2 Robin Platzer; *James Wyeth, Phyllis Wyeth, and Rudolf Nureyev at Elaine's;* 1977; Courtesy Robin Platzer, Twin Images.

It was 1977 in New York City and James Wyeth was introducing his wife Phyllis to his latest model, dancer Rudolf Nureyev. Nureyev arrived at Elaine's restaurant late for dinner and the Wyeths were already seated. Conversation flowed, but a bit uneasily, from ballet to Nureyev's desire to acquire a farm in Virginia. Phyllis and Rudolf were cautious around each other. Finally Phyllis excused herself and reached under the table for the crutches she needed to walk. Nureyev was surprised, not knowing about her accident. He asked her about it and she replied matter-of-factly, "I broke my neck in a car accident when I was twenty-one," then walked away from the table. When she returned, all reticence was gone and Nureyev said to her warmly,

"Never you mind about that. You have lots of spirit and enthusiasm." He saw her strength and admired her for it, but he also encouraged her not to lose sight of the need for "discipline and routine." His words affected her deeply. She credits him for encouraging her to never give up on herself, and she continues to cherish the friendship forged on that day.

Phyllis Wyeth recalls her times with the dancer through the following series of photographs from her personal collection, taken over a thirteen-year period of their friendship. The locations include New York City, the Wyeths's farm in Chadds Ford, Pennsylvania, and St. Petersburg on the occasion of Nureyev's invitational return to dance with the Kirov Ballet.

Fig. 3 Susan Gray; *Nureyev Making Up for* Pierrot Lunaire, *Luigi Pignotti in Background, Uris Theater;* 1977; Courtesy Susan Gray ©/SLPStock.

The day that we met, he asked if I would like to come to the theater the following night. Having never been backstage at the ballet, I was mesmerized watching him prepare. He was applying his own makeup as his masseur, Luigi Pignotti, brought him his tenth cup of tea. He asked, "Luigi, do you have a seat for Phyllis?" Luigi replied that there were no more house seats. Rudolf said, "Put a chair on stage for her." I watched the whole performance from the wings, behind the curtain.

Fig. 4 *Natalia Makarova, Nureyev, Cynthia Gregory, Lucia Chase, Phyllis Wyeth;* c. 1977.

This was a post-performance dinner at the Russian Tea Room. Rudolf sits in the middle, surrounded by women as usual. On his left is Cynthia Gregory who danced the part of the Black Swan in **Swan Lake** *that particular night. Natalia Makarova is on his right, another famous dancer who defected from the Soviet Union shortly after Rudolf. Lucia Chase is seated to my right, the co-founder of the American Ballet Theatre. It was truly exhilarating to be included with such talent.*

Fig. 5 *Martha Graham, Alice Tully, Nureyev, Phyllis Wyeth;* c. 1977.

In this picture we are at the Iranian Embassy speaking with arts patron Alice Tully and modern dance diva, Martha Graham. Rudolf always asked me to join him.

Fig. 6 Douce François Freitas; *Nureyev in King Ludwig's Coat*; c. 1980.

Just like the Wyeths, Rudolf loved costumes! He discovered, in my father-in-law Andrew's collection of many uniforms, a beautiful red embroidered coat that reportedly belonged to King Ludwig of Bavaria. He adored the coat and would wear it every chance he could. He would tease me, "Phyllis, if you get me red coat, I will give you baby." He had a wicked sense of humor and would say things like that just to shock. I am not so easily shocked though, and would say in return, "But Rudolf, I want no baby."

Fig. 7 *Phyllis Wyeth and Nureyev in Carriage*; c. 1977.

Rudolf loved to ride with me in my carriage along the banks of the Brandywine River at our farm in Pennsylvania. He said the trails reminded him of the paths he would walk as a child to his weekly bath in Ufa.

Fig. 8a Phyllis Wyeth; *Nureyev and the Plastic Snakes;* c. 1988.

Rudolf was in Wilmington doing his production of The King and I *over Halloween. Following one performance he asked if he could come over. My young niece and several of her friends were visiting, so I warned him that there was a house full of girls. He came anyway, and joined in the festivities! He judged the girls' pumpkin-carving contest and submitted to being covered with plastic snakes and lizards. This was a side of Rudolf that I do not think many people saw, but he really enjoyed being around kids.*

Fig. 8b Phyllis Wyeth; *Nureyev Judging Pumpkin-Carving Contest for Sophie Mills, Carmen Marin, unidentified friend, Susanna Mitchell, and Lily Stevens;* c. 1988.

Fig. 9 Susan Gray; *Nureyev in Front of* Sable; c. 1988; Courtesy Susan Gray ©/SLPStock.

Here was Rudolf in King Ludwig's coat again at Halloween. The large embroidered cuff fell off the sleeve, so he improvised and stuck it on his head. He was standing in front of Jamie's painting of me in my horse-drawn sleigh, called Sable. *After pondering the painting for a moment, Rudolf said I had such a miserable expression on my face "it looks as though Phyllis was trying to escape Russia."*

Fig. 10 Caroline Alexander Forgason; *The Mariinsky Theater* (St. Petersburg); November 1989.

One of the most enlightening experiences of my life was my trip to St. Petersburg with Rudolf. I had been to Russia two years earlier when the **Three Generations of Wyeth Art** *show traveled there and I became fascinated with the country. I talked to Rudolf when he received the invitation by the Kirov to return. He was distraught because the phone lines were so bad he could not get through to give them an answer. I said to him, "If I can get you through by phone, will you take me with you?" He said he would. As it happened, AT&T had been the sponsor of the* **Three Generations** *show, so I asked my friends for a little assistance.*

I flew over on November 11, 1989. The cover of the **New York Times** *that day showed three hundred thousand people streaming through the Brandenburg Gate in Germany. Rudolf Nureyev would be dancing at the Mariinsky Theater again for the first time since he defected from the Soviet Union in 1961. It was a new world.*

Fig. 11 Caroline Alexander Forgason; *Phyllis Wyeth with Ballerinas, Rehearsal for* La Sylphide; November 1989.

The whole rehearsal space—the mirrors, the barre, the slanted wooden floor with an old watering can to sprinkle on the floor, and the lines of ballerinas—all reminded me of Degas's paintings.

Fig. 12 *Phyllis Wyeth, Nureyev, Tessa Kennedy and Wallace Potts;* 1992.

After Rudolf conducted Romeo and Juliet *in New York, he gave a post-performance party at his apartment. He was so weak that he spent most of the party resting in his bedroom. When he finally emerged I said to him, "Rudolf, if you give up then I will too." He just looked at me knowingly. This is the last time I saw Rudolf.*

Fig. 13 Caroline Alexander Forgason; *Rehearsal for* La Sylphide, *Nureyev and Ayupova;* November 1989.

Rudolf invited me to attend the rehearsals for La Sylphide. *He was to dance the part of James, and his former partner, Ninel Kurgapkina, would lead the rehearsals. She chose twenty-two-year-old Zhanna Ayupova to be the sylph, her first major role. It was fascinating being that close to the creative process.*

Fig. 14 Caroline Alexander Forgason; *Rehearsal for* La Sylphide, *Ayupova and Nureyev;* November 1989.

Fig. 15 Caroline Alexander Forgason; *Phyllis Wyeth and Valentina Savitskaya, Mariinsky Theater;* November 17, 1989.

The Mariinsky was like a jewel, with the blue and gold and magnificent painted ceiling, a place you could only hope to encounter in the most enchanted fairy tale.

Fig. 16 Caroline Alexander Forgason; *Anna Udeltsova and an unidentified friend at the Mariinsky Theater;* November 17, 1989.

The performance at the Kirov was difficult for Rudolf. If his dancing was not all that it had been, the audience did not show it. He received twenty curtain calls, and all the flowers he received were presented to his one-hundred-year-old ballet teacher Anna Udeltsova who started him off at age eleven in Ufa.

Fig. 17 Caroline Alexander Forgason; La Sylphide *by the Kirov Ballet, Nureyev as James, Ayupova as the Sylph;* November 17, 1989.

Although Rudolf longed to dance on the Kirov stage once more, he was plagued with injuries that made his return less than successful. His conflicting sentiments are best expressed in his inscription on a photograph from the performance, "To dear Philiss [sic], this hideous moment in a few years will be the sweetest memory."

After Nureyev's death in 1993, Phyllis reflected on her last moments with him. "I saw him for the last time on May 5, 1992 when he conducted *Romeo and Juliet* in New York." She realized it was only his "force of conviction and drive" that enabled him to continue working. His body had almost completely given out, but his need to stay involved in music and dance was as strong as ever.

Rudolf Nureyev had a power that affected all who knew him. As Phyllis vividly described him, "Nureyev exuded animal energy. His spirit was the spirit of a racehorse with all its beauty and muscle and speed. His body had that perfection. When I watched him dance, his dance was dancing in me. He was my wings, my freedom, my courage. With his departure something departed in me too—much more than just sweet memories."

Fig. 18 Robin Platzer; Rudolf Nureyev,
Curtain Call for *The Sleeping Beauty*;
August 6, 1974; Courtesy Robin
Platzer, Twin Images.

PRESENTING NUREYEV

Barbara Cohen-Stratyner

Photography and the standard ballet repertory have co-existed throughout their histories. Both originated in the early nineteenth century, at first attracting small but devoted audiences. They have grown in popularity and have managed to withstand time and challenges from other artistic and technological forms. Promotional photographs use a code of visual cues to represent dance. This code derives from the movement vocabulary and choreographic syntax of dance. A century and a half of promoting dance through illustrations and photography has made the dancers and the visual code familiar. In this essay I will give readers different ways to look at the photographs of Rudolf Nureyev as they represent his dancing and his experiments with repertory.

Romantic ballet, such as *Giselle* and *La Sylphide,* is the oldest style still represented in the standard repertory. This form of ballet was promoted and illustrated in inexpensive lithography in which content and plot line shared space with depictions of the dancers' skills. The female dancer, portraying a Wili, sylph, or fairy, was often shown in mid-flight or poised on impossibly small pointed feet (see fig. 19). Large-output printing methods soon connected with the promotional needs of the performing arts, which led to an explosion of illustrated programs, broadsides, sheet-music covers, and commercially available portrait prints. Many were second- or third-generation images, based on painted portraits or engravings. It was not necessary for the artist or printer to have actually seen the performance.

Fig. 19 Maria Taglioni in *La Sylphide;* 1836; Hand-colored lithograph after A. E. Chalon, printed by J. Mitchell, London, and Chez Rittner & Grupil, Paris, 1836; Courtesy The New York Public Library for the Performing Arts, Jerome Robbins Dance Division.

Photographers had to share space with the performance—on stage or in a studio. They relied on poses, costumes, or props to connect the person to the performance text. As camera shutter speeds became faster, more attempts were made to portray the skill of dance in motion. The most successful photographs were, again, of the ballerina balanced on pointe in an arabesque, as in this advertisement featuring Anna Pavlova (fig. 20). Male dancers, even acknowledged epitomes of technique like Vaslav Nijinsky, were more often photographed in representation of the plot or atmosphere of the choreography. Experimental photography's quest has been to portray movement. Dance photographers did not focus on horse gaits or bubbles, but looked for the clearest ways to represent motion, and especially motion off the ground.

The uses of these varied illustrations have been remarkably consistent since the early nineteenth century. Most were created to promote the performance within the entertainment industry or to potential ticket buyers. Placement in periodicals could fulfill both functions. For the first third of the century, both newspapers and magazines relied on single-color halftone and rotogravure reproductions, as well as colorized versions of photographs. These adaptations highlighted the best presentation aspects of each technology—the realism and detail of photography with the color intensity of illustration.

Fig. 20 Advertisement for the Welte-Mignon Reproducing Piano, in a Pavlova company tour souvenir program from 1923–24 season; Courtesy The New York Public Library for the Performing Arts, Jerome Robbins Dance Division. The advertisement features both an endorsement and a photograph of Anna Pavlova, as does the advertisement for Baldwin Pianos, on the reverse of this page.

Photographs and photo-reproductions could be used for preview articles and reviews. In the former situation, the image would most often be preselected and provided to the newspaper by the dancers' managers or press representatives. They could be a season old and did not always represent the work as it would be seen. Reviews are still frequently published with a photograph taken at the performance (or dress rehearsal or photo call) that is commissioned and selected by the newspaper.

International dance periodicals have existed since the turn of the twentieth century. They publish articles each month on company seasons, new works, and individual dancers. Articles were illustrated, at the beginning of the century, with halftones, and, since the 1930s, with photographs. Although some magazines have staff photographers, most use images provided by the dance companies or their promotional management. Placement on a magazine cover represents status for the subject, although the composition of the photograph is compromised by text. It is very unusual for a ballet dancer to appear on the cover of a general interest magazine. When Nureyev was featured on both *Time* and *Newsweek* covers in April 1965 (issues of the 16th and 19th respectively), it was seen as the heralding of a golden age for dance.

Dance photographs are also used in publications designed specifically to promote the performance. Daily programs may feature a photograph on the cover, as well as images of the repertory and head shots (close-up portraits) of the members of the company.

Although not specific to dance, the souvenir program has become important for documentation of a season, as well as a collectible. Large-format souvenir programs have been a part of the dance experience since the beginning of the twentieth century. They are published for most companies, major tours, and special events, such as the "Nureyev and Friends" seasons. Since they are developed by the companies for specific seasons, they are a clear indicator of company self-representation. Which performers or works are featured, which dancers are shown in which roles, alphabetical or hierarchy-based listings—all of these factors are illustrated in costumed portraits and action shots. Many souvenir programs since the 1940s have featured single photographers, among them George Platt Lynes for Ballet Theatre and the New York City Ballet, Barbara Morgan for the Martha Graham Company, and Herbert Migdoll for the Joffrey Ballet. Others use a variety of existing performance photographs and commissioned portraits.

Fig. 21 Nureyev and Ninel Kurgapkina in *Swan Lake*; Kirov Ballet press image for the 1962 Hurok tour; Courtesy The New York Public Library for the Performing Arts, Jerome Robbins Dance Division.

Fig. 22 Louis Péres; Nureyev in *The Sleeping Beauty;* 1974; Courtesy The New York Public Library for the Performing Arts, Gift of the photographer, Jerome Robbins Dance Division.

S. Hurok and Hurok Attractions specialized in packaging North American tours for visiting foreign performers and companies in dance and music. Hurok souvenir programs did not feature the work of commissioned photographers, but depended instead on the companies' press stock of images, some of which were not credited to individuals. These souvenir programs represent a shared vision since the Hurok office and the company did not always agree which dancers and works were suitable for the North American audience. There is a curious time warp inherent in the photographs provided by the Kirov for the 1962 Hurok tour. They show Nureyev as the up-and-coming star, but he left the company before it reached America (see fig. 21).

Dance calendars, trading cards, and other collectibles have also featured photographs. Houseworth's Celebrities, San Francisco, published a series in 1866. In my childhood, Capezio sold packs of photo cards along with leotards, tights, and shoes. Dance calendars have also been popular since the 1950s, offering monthly images of companies, works, and performers. Like the Nureyev fan calendars by Jorgen Vollmar, most feature the work of a single photographer.

Many of the photographs shown here are portraits of Nureyev alone or partnering. They were suitable for magazine covers, press photographs, and souvenir programs. The images of Rudolf Nureyev in this exhibit reflect the uses to which they could be put, and also the photographers' desires to present his performances as the best of photography and dance. Because they were taken for publication, these photographs needed not only to represent the dancers' skills, but to give enough visual clues that the viewer can recognize the work and the plot. The selected photographers, the regular corps of those who document ballet in New York and European centers, were actively involved in dance throughout Nureyev's career.

Fig. 23 Linda D. Vartoogian; Nureyev in *Le Corsaire;* 1975; Courtesy The New York Public Library for the Performing Arts, Jerome Robbins Dance Division; Photograph © 1975 Linda D. Vartoogian/FrontRowPhotos, NYC.

The two principal specialties of a male dancer in the standard ballet repertory are elevation, or jumps off the floor while maintaining perfect body placement, and partnering. A standard vocabulary of dance cues developed over the century that allowed photographers to present the technique with enough information to identify works.

For photographing elevation, photographers rely on their knowledge of the repertory. They refer to the practice of placing certain steps and positions at climactic points in choreography. In male solos, which are generally diagonal crosses, photographers try to catch the dancer in the air (see fig. 22). The exhibit includes two frames of these portrayals of elevation—one focusing on the man's variation from *Le Corsaire pas de deux* (recognizable by the feathered head-dress) and one showing Nureyev in a variety of solos in the traditional repertory.

Fig. 25 Janet Levitt; Nureyev in *Swan Lake*, Act I; 1983; Photograph © Janet Levitt.

The photographers, who were also fans, tried to, in the words of Louis Péres, "show respect for the dancers and what they are trying to do." The movements are clean, the body in a continuous line, and the toes pointed. Unlike the romantic ballet lithographs whose sylphs floated in mid-air, the photographers framed the images to include the stage floor as reference, especially in *Le Corsaire*, where Nureyev is alone on stage. Some images, such as Linda D. Vartoogian's *Corsaire* photograph, show us that the leap moved across the stage, covering horizontal space (fig. 23). Fred Fehl's photograph of Nureyev's appearance on the "Bell Telephone Hour" (1962), shows him jumping straight up in the air, parallel to the vertical set pieces around him (fig. 24). In elevation images from *Swan Lake* and *The Sleeping Beauty* he is shown soaring above surrounding dancers (see fig. 25).

Fig. 24 Fred Fehl; Nureyev Performing *Flower Festival at Genzano* on the "Bell Telephone Hour" (NBC TV); January 19, 1962; Courtesy The New York Public Library for the Performing Arts, Walter Terry Estate, Jerome Robbins Dance Division.

To show skill in partnering, knowledgeable photographers could look for either balance or drama. Zoë Dominic's serene photograph of Nureyev and Merle Park in *The Sleeping Beauty* promoted the Royal Ballet's standard of excellence to Hurok's American audience (fig. 26). Photographers looking for more excitement could plan for the "ta-da" poses that appear at the end of most *pas de deux*. Notice, for example, the Nureyev-Fonteyn shoulder lift from *Swan Lake* (Act III) (fig. 27) and the "fish dive" from the Royal Ballet's *The Sleeping Beauty,* in which her extended arms curve in parallel to his leg.

The standard ballet repertory has complex plots with simple emotions. The emotional range for the male lead includes melancholy, love, sorrow, and, in the Soviet repertory, patriotism. Some poses transcend the specific *mise en scène* but specify

Fig. 27 Roy Round; Nureyev and Margot Fonteyn in *Swan Lake;* c. 1976; Black Swan *pas de deux,* as performed by the Royal Ballet; Courtesy The New York Public Library for the Performing Arts, Jerome Robbins Dance Division.

emotion. In the performance photographs of the Nureyev-Fonteyn partnership that Hurok Attractions used to promote Royal Ballet tours, it is frequently deep love. See, for example, the images of them in press shots of *Romeo and Juliet* and *Marguerite and Armand* (fig. 28). These photographs actually show eye contact between the dancers, but the poses and plot lines suggest romance. In photographs of them in rehearsal, the message is of enjoyable hard work.

Fig. 26 Zoë Dominic; Nureyev and Merle Park in *The Sleeping Beauty,* Act II, with the Royal Ballet; c.1966; Courtesy The New York Public Library for the Performing Arts, Jerome Robbins Dance Division.

Some visual cues rely on *mise en scène*, costuming, or hand props. Nijinsky's *L'Après-midi d'un Faune* is always recognizable by the Léon Bakst costumes, although over sixty years separates its premiere from the Nureyev revival (fig. 29). Jerome Robbins's *Afternoon of the Faun,* to the same score, is performed in rehearsal clothes and offers no costume clues, but is a work that can be recognized from pose and focus. Set in a rehearsal studio, the dancers continually look at their reflections in the imaginary mirror at the fourth wall. Photographs of Act II of *Giselle* frequently show the same iconic pose, an unusual partnered arabesque in which Albrecht kneels in front of Giselle who, by balancing into an arabesque, seems to forgive him his betrayal. Poses in George Balanchine's *Apollo* are unique and so well known that they have developed names. The triple arabesque is known as "troika," after the Russian carriage.

A selection of dance photographs can reveal the sightlines and

perspective of their creators. Sightlines refer to the actual angle of vision at which they are taken. Most of Nureyev's performances took place in large, proscenium-oriented spaces, such as the Royal Opera House, Covent Garden, the Metropolitan Opera House, or Broadway theaters, and were designed and choreographed for such spaces. With few exceptions, the photographers were in the audience, seated in the orchestra slightly below the stage or in balcony boxes, above and to the side of the stage. They shared the same visual access and sightline as the audience.

When a photographer breaks the traditional sightlines, the viewer is given access to the secrets of performance. Martha Swope took such a photograph of Nureyev's New York debut at the Brooklyn Academy of Music, in 1962 (fig. 30). Not only was she in the wings, but she photographed the dancers and Academy staff members in the opposite wings watching him in wonder.

Those proscenium-oriented spaces, and most of the designers who create wing-and-drop scenery, scenic

Fig. 28 Nureyev and Fonteyn in *Marguerite and Armand* (chor. Ashton), Royal Ballet; 1963; Courtesy The New York Public Library for the Performing Arts, Jerome Robbins Dance Division.

Fig. 29 Photograph by Herbert Migdoll © 1979; Nureyev in *L'Après-midi d'un Faune* (Joffrey revival); 1979; Courtesy The New York Public Library for the Performing Arts, Jerome Robbins Dance Division.

Fig. 30 Martha Swope; Nureyev's NYC Debut in *Don Quixote* at the Brooklyn Academy of Music; 1962; Courtesy TimePix.

pieces, and lighting for them, are based in the standard perspective in the Euro-American art tradition. Choreographers reflect it by placing major characters and actions in the center foreground. Lev Ivanov, choreographer of the "white" acts (II and IV) of *Swan Lake,* was the great master of audience focus. Background dancers, especially *corps de ballet* in identical costumes, are arranged in lines and groupings to focus the audience onto the important activity. Solos and climactic *pas de deux* are placed in the sweet spot at center stage. Audiences are trained to see in this tradition, and most photographers reflect it. Through the first half of the exhibit, you can see lines of swans and groupings of peasants and courtiers guiding your eyes toward Nureyev.

As Nureyev expanded his repertory, he took on new forms of movement. The photographers who created the images, and the press and management staff that selected them, now had three responsibilities. They had to represent Nureyev as a great dancer, to represent the works as they were created, and to represent the impact of the expanded repertory. The photographers had one great advantage—they often knew the modern dance and experimental ballet repertories well and were able to adapt to an appropriate new scheme of visual cues.

The first, most obvious change to look for in these photographs is the lack of shoes. Through decades of stratification in the dance world, the foremost identity clue was that ballet is performed in slippers and modern dance is not. Robin Platzer's photograph of Nureyev's triumphant curtain call after *Aureole* was published in *People* magazine as proof that he could dance barefoot (fig. 31). The shift in *mise en scène* is also obvious. Neither Isamu Noguchi sculpture nor Zabar's shopping bags are to be found in *Swan Lake*. The painted wing-and-drop scenery has disappeared. There are bare stages, abstract scaffolding, and works set in rehearsal studios.

One new challenge involved presenting the evolving specialties of the male dancer as found in the movement vocabulary of the experimental ballet repertory. The London photographers who covered the Royal Ballet were the first to document this. The images of Roland Petit's *Paradise Lost,* provided for the 1967 Hurok tour of the Royal Ballet, portray ballet's most famous partnership in an anti-ballet. Fonteyn seems completely secure in stridently un-orthodox holds, suspended between Nureyev's knees or balancing an arabesque on his finger, while he rolls over on his back. Through guest appearances with European companies, Nureyev

Fig. 31 Robin Platzer; Nureyev, Curtain Call for Paul Taylor's *Aureole;* 1974; Courtesy Robin Platzer, Twin Images.

Fig. 32 Louis Péres; Nureyev in Martha Graham's *El Penitente*; c. 1980; Courtesy Louis Péres.

became more comfortable with works that integrated movement and complex dramatic situations. Photographers documented these radical departures from conventional partnering. In John Neumeier's *Don Juan,* Nureyev does not provide respectfully invisible supports for a ballerina's arabesque. In one pose, he restrains Mary Jago's upper arms; in the other, he holds Vanessa Harwood by her neck.

Nureyev needed to learn the challenging movement vocabulary of American modern dance. When Nureyev and Fonteyn first performed with Martha Graham's company, much of the press attention went to the costumes by Halston and the presence of then First Lady Betty Ford. Nureyev focused on Graham's syntax of movement, which is centered in the torso. It is based in gravity, the traditional enemy of the ballet dancer, and represented by the dancer's relationship to the ground. The photographers, most of whom regularly documented modern dance, knew how to frame the dancer in the alternate vocabulary. Beverley Vawter Gallegos's image of Lucifer seems to show him crushed between the Noguchi sculpture and the stage floor. Louis Péres's photograph of *El Penitente* represents the force of gravity by catching the dancer in the midst of upward momentum (fig. 32).

Nureyev's expanded repertory also featured elevation. Modern dance jumps are at least as difficult as ballet leaps. Jack Vartoogian's photograph of *Moments* uses appropriate framing devices by showing Nureyev above the floor, chest height to an onlooking dancer (fig. 33). It is unquestionably represented as a modern dance jump because his limbs are crooked, his gaze focused on the floor, and the movement straight up into a stag leap.

Nureyev himself was known as a tough judge of his own representation and his own dancing. More than one photographer has said that he ripped up prints that displeased him. But he was also generous in his praise if an image showed that everything was placed correctly. He had a keen awareness of photographs as they presented his talent and his changing repertory to the world.

Fig. 33 Jack Vartoogian; Nureyev and Bill Hollahan in *Moments* (Murray Louis); 1976; Courtesy The New York Public Library for the Performing Arts, Jerome Robbins Dance Division; Photograph © 1978 Jack Vartoogian/FrontRowPhotos, NYC.

Nureyev Revisited

James Wyeth's Portraits

Lauren Raye Smith

Rarely in art history has a model and artist relationship continued and evolved years after the model's death. James Wyeth first met Rudolf Nureyev in New York City in 1974. He was instantly intrigued with the dancer, so much so that Nureyev has continued to inspire him artistically for twenty-four years. In 1977, Wyeth created over thirty finely rendered, small-scale portraits of him. These intimate studies primarily focus on the subtleties of Nureyev's expressive face and physical presence. In 1993, following the dancer's death, Wyeth returned to several large scale, three-quarter figure studies that he had begun earlier, and reworked them with an energy and vitality that recalled the dancer in life. The 2001 portraits show Wyeth's evolution as a painter and also reflect on Nureyev as a dancer.

Nureyev was both championed and criticized in his field largely because he defied easy classification. Many critics and choreographers of the time condemned Nureyev for his star quality, arguing that when he was on stage the audience did not notice any other dancers. However, it was this same charisma that drew a new and diverse audience to the ballet. Although temperamentally very different, Wyeth and Nureyev found common ground; each was obsessed with his craft. Both artists started with traditional training before finding their own, more interpretive methods of expression. It would take several years for the busy dancer to agree to pose for the painter, but the series of portraits that Wyeth created of Nureyev is an in-depth physical and psychological study of this intriguing personality.

While in New York, Wyeth was invited by his friend, pop artist Andy Warhol, to work in his Broadway studio known as "The Factory." Wyeth and Warhol, who came from seemingly different backgrounds, completed portraits of each other in 1976 and exhibited together in a show called *Portraits of Each Other* that traveled from New York to Pennsylvania, Tennessee, and Monaco. In the 1970s, Warhol was cultivating celebrities for his own portrait work and so, in 1977, he encouraged Wyeth to work on his portrait of Arnold Schwarzenegger at the Factory, too. It was at this time that Wyeth became reacquainted with Nureyev and the dancer finally agreed to pose, but not in the Factory. Warhol had photographed Nureyev a few years earlier during an unsuccessful, tension-filled interview for *Interview* magazine. Nureyev, even more than most celebrities, was extremely sensitive about his appearance and had torn up the Polaroids and refused to ever step foot in Warhol's studio.[1]

Fig. 34 *Profile with Black Wash Background, Head, Nureyev (Study #23);* 1977; Combined Mediums; 20 3/4 x 21 1/4;
Collection of Philip and Tina DeNormandie.

J. WYETH

Fig. 35 *Full Face and Partial Chest, Head, Nureyev (Study #10);* 1977; Combined Mediums; 16 x 20; Collection of the Artist.
(detail, front cover and frontispiece)

To Wyeth, the dichotomies in the dancer's character were fascinating. He recalled:

What attracted me was Nureyev's physicality, that peasant force. He is very aware of his animal nature— he has this marvelous energy, and he is always moving, always on stage. He is as strange off the dance stage as on.[2]

Wyeth was well known for his portraits of animals as well as for his portraits of celebrities, and he found the perfect melding of both in Nureyev. The dancer had a dangerous, feral quality about him, and an infamous temper that could flare, then just as quickly disappear. Yet there was also a sweet, childlike aspect to the dancer that was evident to those who knew him well. He felt at home only on stage; he often lived in hotel rooms or stayed with friends, even in cities where he owned a home.

In the 1977 works Wyeth focused on personality traits, or the dancer's face and body structure, as opposed to ballet movements. The "studies" do not necessarily build to a final definitive portrait; they are portraits in and of themselves. The exploratory nature of these works is evidenced by the common occurrence of multiple images on one page. Many of the head studies, such as *Profile with Black Wash Background, Head, Nureyev (Study #23)* (fig. 34), and *Full Face and Partial Chest, Head, Nureyev (Study #10)* (fig. 35) have ghostly sketches of partial faces, or just eyes, in various orientations on the same page. Wyeth used the color of the support, whether it was tan-toned board in the smaller studies, or brown cardboard in the larger ones, as the midtone for flesh. He then built the figure with white highlights and dark washes or charcoal. Without excess of detail, Wyeth suggested both form and texture. He indicated the fur in *Profile, In Fur, Nureyev (Study #9)* (fig. 36) by using both the soft end and the handle of the paintbrush. He laid in the fuzziness of the outline of the coat, and then added highlights to the dark washes by scratching them in with the brush handle. Although he was using simply a pencil line to suggest the coat in *Unfinished Coat, In Fur, Nureyev (Study #13)* (fig. 37) the viewer is given enough visual information to feel the weight of the coat on Nureyev's shoulders. As Wyeth said of his portraiture:

> There's no formula to it. Sometimes it can be a momentary look that's a distillation of all these different moods. But I'm never satisfied with one portrait. I think the studies probably are as important as the finished piece.[3]

He explained why he did not, at this time, depict the dancer in motion: "At the time I was working on the studies of Nureyev I became so fascinated with him as a person, that the fact that he was dancing was almost immaterial."[4] The series of heads also explores the expressive quality of Nureyev's strong Tatar features (see figs. 38–41). He was an actor as well as a dancer and could convey great emotion with only a subtle change in his face. The slightly raised eyebrow and lowered eyelids in *Three-Quarter Face Vertical, Head, Nureyev (Study #24)* (fig. 42) are suggestive of a certain attitude.

Wyeth recognized that he could not separate the dancer from dance, however, and he spent a great deal of time observing Nureyev in rehearsals and in performance. Wyeth described watching Nureyev prepare for a performance (see fig. 43):

> It was the most incredible sort of Dr. Jekyll thing. He started doing these dance movements, warming up . . . but it's more of a mental thing than a physical thing. He was psyching himself. Dance has a silence . . . there was no music, just his breathing and the thumping of his feet. Then behind the heavy curtain you start to hear the house coming in and the orchestra warming up, and here would be this creature in white makeup. Occasionally he would look at me but I could tell he wasn't seeing anything; he was totally immersed in it. . . . Finally he'd reach this sort of pitch, sweat pouring off him, and he'd walk off stage, go to his dressing room. It was unbelievable.[5]

Wyeth's early training gave him the skills to render the dancer's body with accuracy. His first formal lessons were with his aunt, Carolyn, a respected painter herself. She had taken over the studio of her father, N. C. Wyeth, and continued his tradition of teaching. James spent two years learning the basics of drawing, each day drawing cubes, spheres, and cones in charcoal. "I think it was to instill some discipline," he recalled. "If I was going to paint I really better buckle down."[6] He also commented, "It's wonderful to have that background and to have those skills at your fingertips. Then you can charge off in whichever directions you want."[7]

Fig. 36 *Profile, In Fur, Nureyev (Study #9)*; 1977; Combined Mediums; 20 x 16; Collection of Mr. and Mrs. Andrew Wyeth.

Following the tradition of painter and educator Thomas Eakins, Wyeth spent two months at a Harlem hospital morgue working with a Russian anatomist dissecting cadavers and sketching the inner workings of the human body. Eakins, an artist Wyeth has cited as influential on his own work, was considered a "radical" instructor at the Pennsylvania Academy of the Fine Arts in the 1880s for his use of nude models and his lectures on anatomy illustrated by dissections performed in front of the students. Eakins believed that, "to study anatomy out of a book is like learning to paint out of a book. It's a waste of time."[8] Of the experience at the morgue, Wyeth says, "When I draw a person's cheek, I know what's under that. I actually took that apart and felt that muscle and felt the various bone structures. That I'll never forget."[9] Wyeth's sketches of Nureyev often included measurements such as "calf is 2 widths of ankle" or "shoulder (outside) is 4 wrists," an indication of the importance of structural accuracy as a basis in his work (see figs. 45–47).

Although Nureyev was one of the most photographed dancers of the time, Wyeth felt there were aspects of the dancer that had not been seen and could not be captured with photography (see figs. 48–51). Wyeth commented, "I spent hours just watching Nureyev practice, and did hundreds . . . of studies of him, purely because I was dying to record him. He was enigmatic, a very complex individual."[10] Of his portraiture in general, Wyeth says:

When I work on a portrait, it's really osmosis. I try to become the person I'm painting. A successful portrait isn't about the sitter's physical characteristics—his nose, eyeballs and whatnot—but more the mood and the overall effect. I try not to impose anything of mine on him. I try to get to the point where, if the sitter painted, he'd paint a portrait just the way I'm doing it.[11]

What he imposes on his sitters, however, is his artist's vision for what makes that person an individual, another indication of the influence of Eakins. A quote referring to Eakins's portraits could describe the younger artist's work as well:

J. WYETH

Fig. 40 *Three-Quarter Face Horizontal, Head, Nureyev (Study #26)*; 1977; Combined Mediums; 16 x 20; Collection of the Artist.

Fig. 41 *Double Image, Head, Nureyev (Study #21)*; 1977; Combined Mediums; 20 x 16; Collection of the Artist.

Fig. 42 *Three-Quarter Face Vertical, Head, Nureyev (Study #24)*; 1977; Combined Mediums; 20 x 16; Collection of the Artist.

Fig. 43 *Head and Chest, In Fur, Nureyev (Study #1)*; 1977; Combined Mediums; 16 x 20; Unlocated; Photo Courtesy of the Artist.

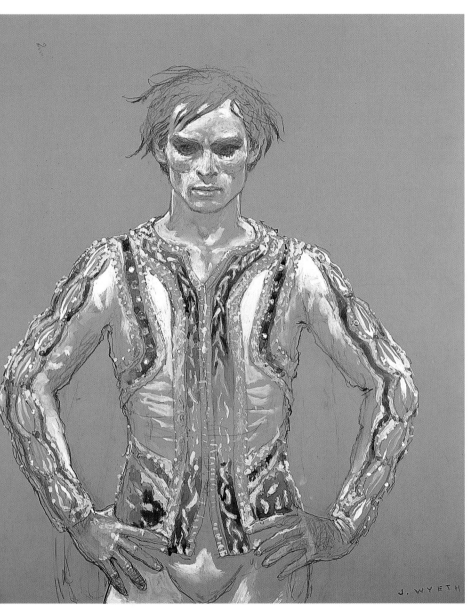

Fig. 44 *Portrait of Rudolf Nureyev—Dress Rehearsal/Raymonda*; 1977;
Combined Mediums; 20 x 16; Collection of the Artist.

While the average tendency is to soften and reduce to the normal, his was the opposite: to concentrate on the individual traits that made the sitter a person like no other in the world, and to picture them with uncompromising saliency and boldness. His likenesses lay below the surface, in the construction of the head, which is always felt beneath the flesh; while the features, even the texture of the skin, were depicted with the same unerring accuracy.[12]

Nureyev was Wyeth's most difficult model. Although Nureyev had agreed to pose for the portrait, Wyeth found it nearly impossible to get the busy dancer to interrupt his schedule for the sittings. Wyeth recalled, in desperation, asking another dancer with a similar frame to stand in for the initial studies. Nureyev was highly sensitive about the way his body was portrayed. He was enraged when he found out about the substitute model and he began regularly scheduled sittings immediately. Wyeth noted, "If I did a drawing of his toe, he wanted to see if it was correct. Finally we had this great argument and I had to explain, 'Rudolf, you're interpretive in your dance and many of these drawings are interpretive, too.'"[13]

Wyeth arrived at the pose and the use of the fur coat for many of the studies and for *Portrait of Rudolf Nureyev* by watching the dancer's natural actions. When at rest, the dancer would often stand as Wyeth depicted him, with both hands on hips and shoulders slightly forward, weight shifted to one leg (see figs. 52–53). Wyeth explained:

> Using the fur coat was pretty much my fantasy of Nureyev and his Russian background. He does not wear a fur coat while he's dancing, so he got very upset when I did that. It was clearly my interpretation, and I took certain liberties with the portrait.[14]

The dancer's acceptance of Wyeth's "interpretation" initially seems unusual given his reputation, but in fact, Nureyev would often throw on his fur coat and leave the theater in full stage makeup. In the oil painting *Portrait of Rudolf Nureyev* (fig. 54), Wyeth depicts Nureyev at the rehearsal barre in his fur coat. He looks slightly downward, as if the viewer were seated on the floor, a subordinate position. The lighting, as well as his expression, is softer than in many of the studies, and he appears at ease with his role as the center of attention.

The painter had explored the idea of Nureyev wearing a fur hat in addition to the coat, but set aside the studies before completion (see fig. 55). He recently returned to these unfinished studies for *Portrait of Nureyev* (fig. 56), which he completed in 2001. The dark background is punctuated by the line of klieg lights and Nureyev's face in white makeup, which appears even more ghostly with the contrast of his red lips and slightly red-rimmed eyes. His untamed, animalistic nature is implied by the fact that he is enveloped in fur; his look is distant but intense.

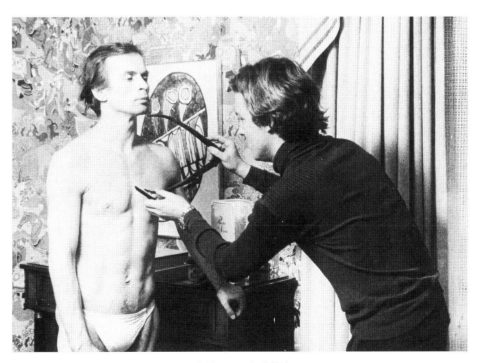

Fig. 45 Michael McKenzie; *James Wyeth Measuring Rudolf Nureyev*; 1977; Photograph © Michael McKenzie.

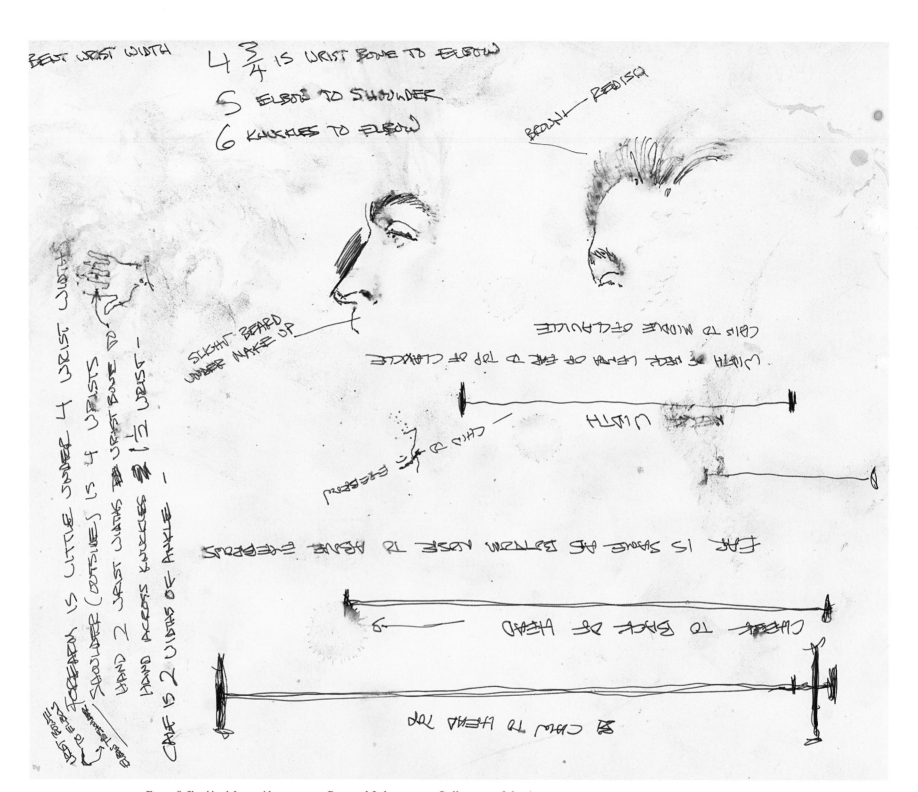

Fig. 46 *Sketchbook Image, N-31a;* 1977; Pen and Ink; 11 x 14; Collection of the Artist.

Fig. 47 *Sketchbook Image, N-33*; 1977; Pen and Ink; 11 x 14; Collection of the Artist.

Wyeth's works often feature and enhance the most surreal qualities of his subjects. An avid collector of toys, in the late 1970s Wyeth purchased an automaton of a clown seated on a crescent moon (fig. 57). The clown's face reminded the painter of Nureyev in *Pierrot Lunaire,* the Glen Tetley ballet that was part of the program during the 1977 "Nureyev and Friends" season—the same year he was posing for Wyeth. As Pierrot, Nureyev appeared in white face makeup. In 1979, Wyeth conflated the toy clown and Nureyev in his stage makeup to create a painting called *Automaton* (fig. 59; see also fig. 58). This painting, along with several of the portraits of Nureyev, was part of an exhibition of the work of the three generations of Wyeth painters that toured internationally in 1987. When the exhibition appeared at the Academy of the Arts of the USSR, St. Petersburg, and the Academy of the Arts of the USSR, Moscow, Soviet sentiment against Nureyev and his defection was still strong. His portraits were removed from the show. Russian officials allowed *Automaton* to be shown in the country, to the amusement of the painter and the dancer. Two years later, after the fall of Communism, Nureyev himself was invited back to St. Petersburg to dance with his first dance company, the Kirov Ballet.

Following Nureyev's death in 1993, Wyeth discovered several unfinished studies in his studio. He went back to four of the three-quarter figure studies that he had begun in 1977 and reworked them, referring to the reworking as a sort of closure. Stylistically, his work had become more expressive in the 1990s. He added strong white highlights to the figures that were not necessarily descriptive of form, but conveyed a sense of the dancer's power and energy. When viewed together, *White Highlights, Three-Quarter Figure, Nureyev (Study #15)* (fig. 60), and *Black Background, Three-Quarter Figure, Nureyev (Study #17)* (fig. 61) complement each other, like a photographic negative and positive, or perhaps the yin and yang of the dancer's personality. In *Nude, Three-Quarter Figure, Nureyev (Study #18)* (fig. 62) the dancer is fully exposed yet unselfconscious. The viewer is directed by the strong lighting to Nureyev's face and upper body. *Yellow Leotard, Three-Quarter Figure, Nureyev (Study #16)* (fig. 63) varies from the other three in pose and color. The yellow leotard and the full stage makeup are the intended focus of this work. Wyeth has even written a reminder to himself in the upper left corner, "White makeup on eyelashes!!"

Fig. 48 *Full Face, Torso, Nureyev (Study #5)*; 1977; Combined Mediums;
16 x 20; Collection of Dr. and Mrs. David A. Skier.

Fig. 49 *Unfinished Hand, Torso, Nureyev (Study #92)*; 1977;
Combined Mediums; (sight) 18 3/4 x 15 1/2;
Collection of Mr. and Mrs. Stephen H. Casey.

J. WYETH

Fig. 50 *Black Leotard,*
Nureyev (Study #3);
1977; Combined
Mediums; 20 x 16;
Private Collection.

Fig. 51 *Black Wash Background, Torso, Nureyev (Study #14)*; 1977; Combined Mediums; 16 1/2 x 20 1/2;
Collection of the Brandywine River Museum.

Still inspired by Nureyev eight years after the dancer's death, Wyeth completed a series of boldly colored large-scale works in 2001 (see fig. 64). Nureyev is depicted as the world knew him, as a dancer on stage, but with a vision that has evolved since Wyeth's 1977 portraits. The painter commented, "That was his life—performance. But in life he was such a strong force, he was so captivating, it was hard to focus on what he was doing. Now, of course, the distance helps me see him in context."[15] These paintings have a fanciful, otherworldly quality to them. They possess less of the physical solidity of the 1977 pieces, but a greater sense of drama and fantasy, exemplified by *Nureyev—Swan Lake* (fig. 65). Nureyev as the prince, as he was so often cast, dances in a star-studded purple sky. Although there are shadows beneath his feet, he does not seem to touch the earth. An ethereal glow appears to emanate from within the dancer in both *Nureyev—Don Quixote—White Background* (fig. 66) and *Nureyev—Don Quixote—Yellow Background* (fig. 67). The gesture and movement take precedence over the dancer himself; his personality no longer eclipses his dancing. For *Mort de Noureev* (fig. 68), Wyeth drew inspiration from famous death scenes such as the one in *Romeo and Juliet.* Two ballerinas who recall the dancers of Degas hide their faces and grieve for the fallen prince. This theatrical homage to Nureyev has a slightly unsettling quality. Warm yellow light bathes the stage, yet the spotlights on the dancer make him appear cold and white.

Wyeth's most successful works often involve a subject he has worked with repeatedly, as with Nureyev. He has mastered the exterior form and the surface detail, and is free to allow the subject to expand with his own imagination (see fig. 69). In Wyeth's words:

> What's exciting is the continuity. You're getting closer and closer. Doing a series allows me to concentrate on how a subject evolved and how it affects me. The end result is sort of the by-product. People always say, "How do you know when the thing is finished?" Well, nothing is ever finished. . . . At times, I could work on a painting for the rest of my life.[16]

Fig. 52 *Full-Length Study for Portrait of Rudolf Nureyev (Study #19)*; 1977; Combined Mediums; 48 x 36; Collection of MBNA America.

Fig. 53 *Hands On Hips, In Fur, Nureyev (Study #25)*; 1977; Combined Mediums; 35 1/2 x 45 3/4; Unlocated;
Photo Courtesy of the Artist.

Fig. 54 *Portrait of Rudolf Nureyev*; 1977;
Oil on Canvas; 45 1/4 X 40 1/2;
Collection of Arturo and Holly Melosi;
Photo Courtesy of the Artist.

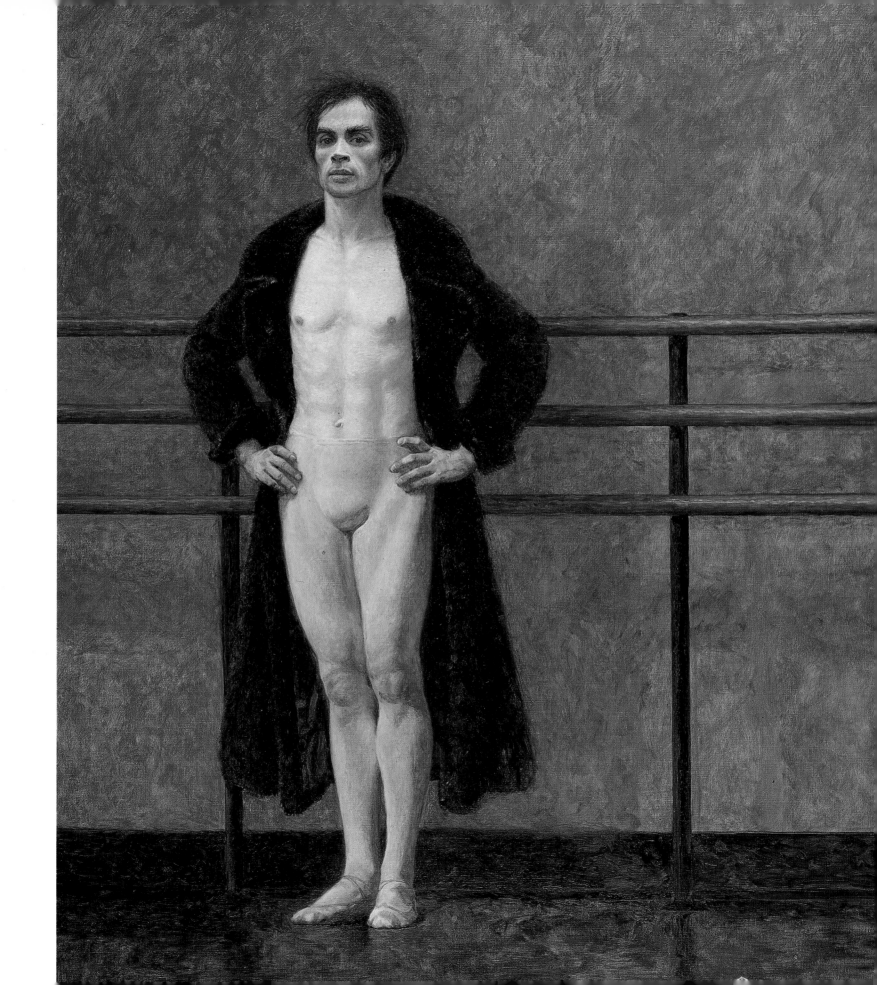

Fig. 55 *Study for Portrait of Nureyev;* 1977; Combined Mediums; 16 x 20; Collection of the Artist.

Notes

1. Bob Colacello, *Holy Terror: Andy Warhol Close Up* (New York: Harper Collins, 1990), 107–9.
2. Phil Patton, "Painting's Favorite Son," *United Mainliner,* October 1980, 112.
3. Sandra Carpenter and Greg Schaber, "Jamie Wyeth: His Art and Insights," *The Artist's Magazine,* August 1997, 38.
4. James Wyeth, interview by Lauren Raye Smith, 31 August 2001.
5. Ibid.
6. Joyce Hill Stoner, "Jamie Wyeth: Masked Master of Sensuous Surfaces," in *A Closer Look* (Wilmington: Delaware Art Museum, 1998), 30.
7. Gordon Wetmore, "Jamie Wyeth: Painter of Patriots, Presidents, Seagulls and the White House," *International Artist,* April/May 2001, 49.
8. Lloyd Goodrich, *Thomas Eakins: His Life and Work* (New York: Whitney Museum of American Art, 1933), 77.
9. Scott Heiser, "Down on the Farm with Jamie Wyeth," *Interview,* February 1974, 12.
10. Carpenter and Schaber, "Jamie Wyeth," 37.
11. Ibid., 38.
12. Goodrich, *Thomas Eakins,* 113.
13. "How Jamie Wyeth Paints People," *Art and Man* 8, no. 5 (March 1978): 5.
14. Ibid.
15. Jamie Wyeth, interview by Lauren Raye Smith, 31 August 2001.
16. Carpenter and Schaber, "Jamie Wyeth," 39.

Fig. 56 *Portrait of Nureyev;* 1977/2001; Combined Mediums; 32 x 40; Collection of Jim and Jocelyn Stewart. (detail p. 10)

Fig. 57 Automaton toy; Collection of James Wyeth.

Fig. 58 *Automaton, Study #1;* 1979; Combined Mediums; 12 1/4 x 8 1/4; Collection of the Artist.

Fig. 59 *Automaton*; 1979; Oil on Canvas; 34 1/2 x 29 1/4; Collection of Mr. and Mrs. Frank E. Fowler.

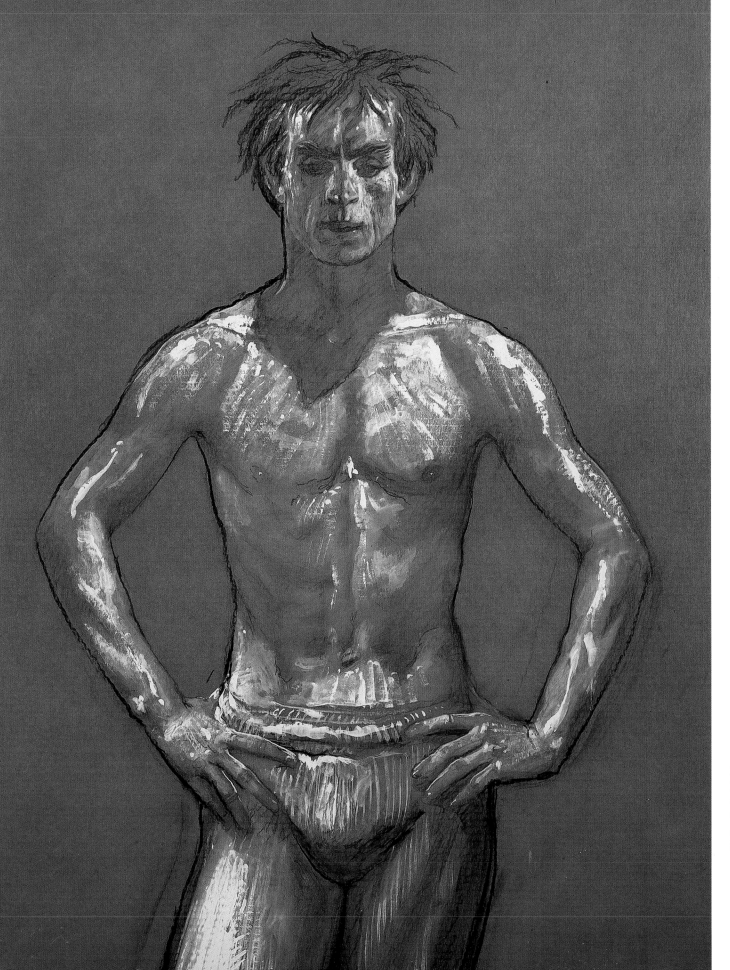

Fig. 60 *White Highlights,*
Three-Quarter Figure, Nureyev
(Study #15); 1977/1993;
Combined Mediums;
48 x 36; Collection of
the Artist.

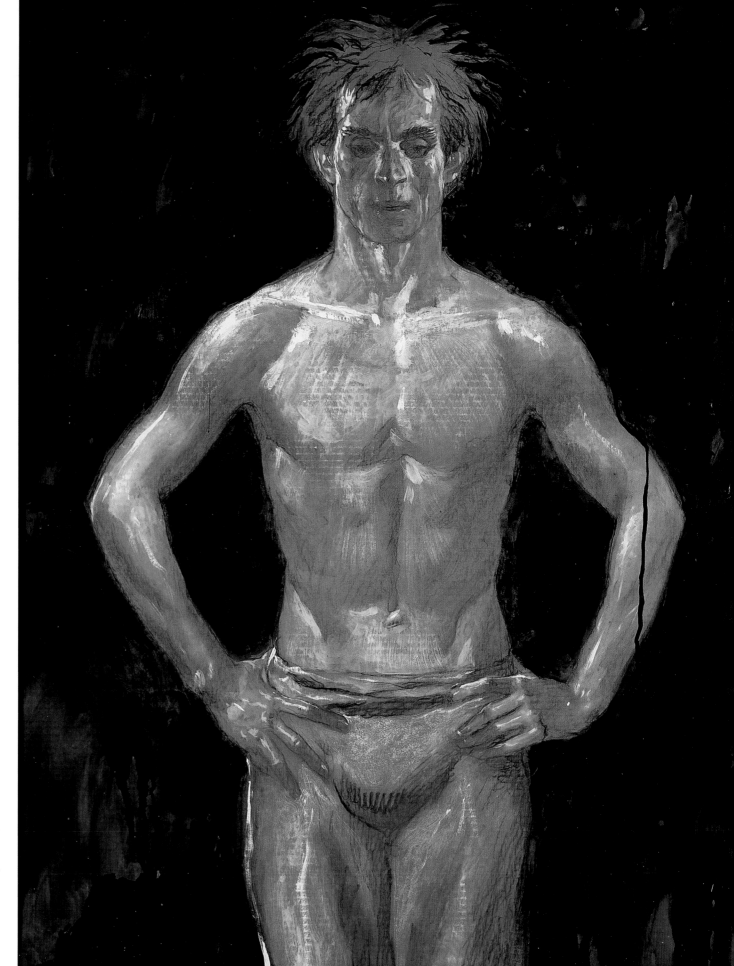

Fig. 61 *Black Background,
Three-Quarter Figure, Nureyev
(Study #17)*; 1977/1993;
Combined Mediums;
48 x 36; Collection of
the Artist. (detail p. 39)

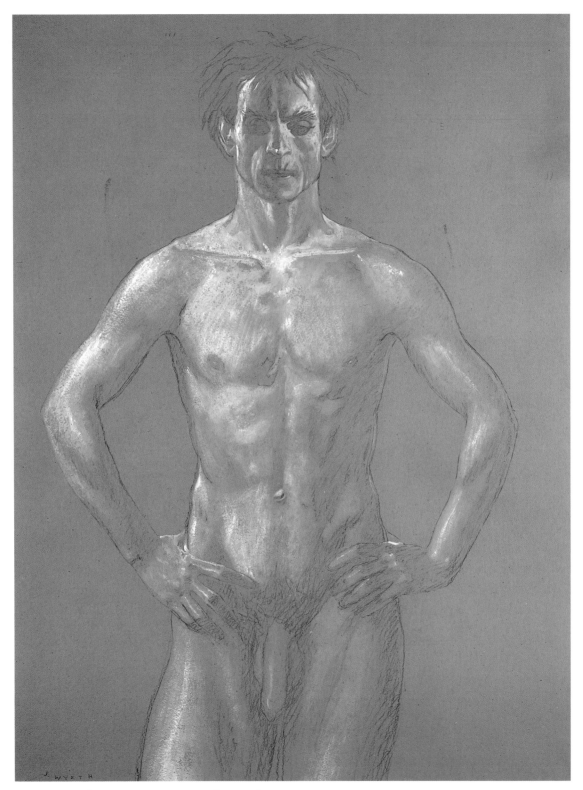

Fig. 62 *Nude, Three-Quarter Figure, Nureyev (Study #18)*; 1977/1993; Combined Mediums;
48 x 34 1/2; Collection of the Artist.

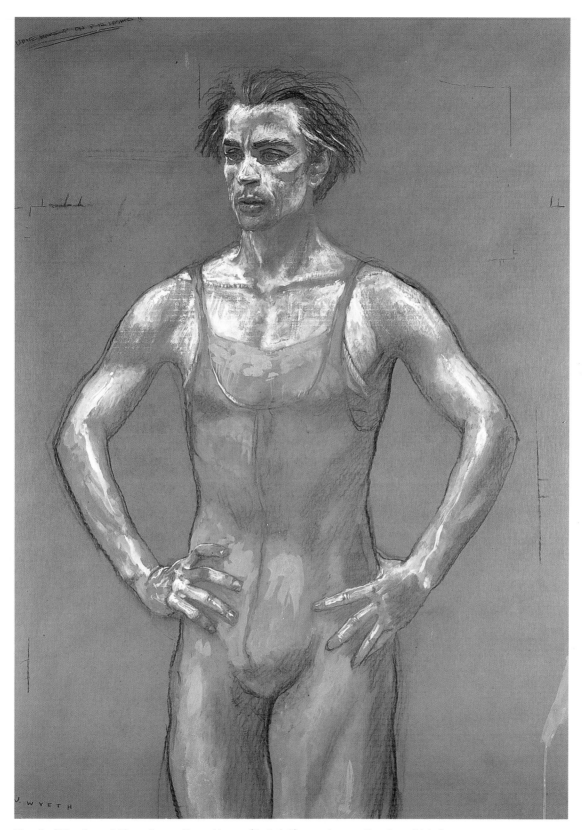

Fig. 63 *Yellow Leotard, Three-Quarter Figure, Nureyev (Study #16)*; 1977/1993; Combined Mediums; 48 x 36; Collection of Dr. Charles Ansbacher and Ambassador Swanee Hunt.

Fig. 64 *Nureyev—Purple Scarf*; 2001;
Combined Mediums; 35 1/2 x 25 1/2;
Collection of the Artist. (detail p. 40)

Fig. 65 *Nureyev—Swan Lake;* 2001;
Combined Mediums; 48 x 30;
Collection of the Artist.

Fig. 66 *Nureyev—Don Quixote—White Background;* 2001; Combined Mediums; 30 1/2 x 37;
Collection of the Artist.

Fig. 67 *Nureyev—Don Quixote—Yellow Background;* 2001; Combined Mediums; 47 3/4 x 36; Collection of the Artist.

Fig. 68 *Mort de Noureev*; 2001; Combined Mediums; 42 1/2 x 78; Collection of the Artist.

Fig. 69 *Curtain Call*; 2001;
Combined Mediums;
80 x 60;
Collection of the Artist.

Selected Chronology of James Wyeth

1946

6 July. James Browning Wyeth born in Wilmington, Delaware to Andrew Newell Wyeth (b. 1917) and Betsy James Wyeth (b. 1921). James, known as Jamie, has one brother, Nicholas (b. 1943).

1959

Leaves school in seventh grade, against the wishes of the Pennsylvania School Board, to devote himself to painting. He is tutored in academic subjects in the mornings and spends afternoons in formal study of drawing with Carolyn Wyeth, his aunt.

1961

Completes first oil of a friend, Jimmy Lynch, *The Soldier* (Stuart Kingston Galleries, Delaware). Works primarily on watercolor landscapes of Brandywine Valley and Maine, where family spends summers.

Completes: *Luke* (private collection).

1963

Explores portraiture in oil.

First acquisition by a museum, *The Capstan,* 1963, (Farnsworth Art Museum).

Completes: *Shorty* (Collection of Mr. and Mrs. Andrew Wyeth), *Lester* (private collection),

Portrait of Helen Taussig (Johns Hopkins University—commissioned by the University), *Mushroom Picker* (private collection).

1964

Family friend, actor Robert Montgomery, commissions portrait.

Completes: *The Axe* (private collection), *Record Player* (private collection), *Halloween* (private collection), *Portrait of Deo duPont Weymouth* (private collection), *Portrait of Hamalainen* (private collection).

1965

Enlists in the Delaware Air National Guard, attending boot camp in Amarillo, Texas.

Studies with Russian anatomist at morgue in New York City for two months, dissecting and drawing cadavers.

Paints portrait of New York City Ballet founder and family friend, Lincoln Kirstein.

Meets other artists with whom he will later work, including Andy Warhol.

Completes: *Portrait of Lincoln Kirstein* (National Portrait Gallery, gift of Lincoln Kirstein), *Draft Age* (Brandywine River Museum).

1966

First one-man show, *James Wyeth Paintings,* Knoedler Gallery, New York City. (Lincoln Kirstein writes foreword to exhibition catalogue.)

Declines commission from Kennedy family for portrait of President John F. Kennedy. Decides to complete portrait on his own. Befriends Jacqueline and other members of family. Sketches brothers, Robert and Edward, as reference for final portrait.

Completes: *Portrait of Jeffrey* (private collection), *The Squall* (private collection), *Portrait of Governor Charles L. Terry, Jr.* (Bureau of Museums, State of Delaware—completed as part of his duty for Delaware Air National Guard), *Bronze Age* (Farnsworth Art Museum).

1967

Exhibits works at National Gallery of Art, Washington, D.C.; participating artist in the "Eyewitness to Space" program sponsored by NASA (other participants included Lamar Dodd, Peter Hurd, Robert Rauschenberg, and Andy Warhol).

Completes: *Portrait of President John F. Kennedy* (private collection).

1968

Purchases house built by artist Rockwell Kent on Monhegan Island, Maine, and begins spending summers there. Focuses on landscapes of island.

11 December. Marries Phyllis Mills.

Completes: *Portrait of Lady* (private collection), *Island Roses* (Collection of Mr. and Mrs. Andrew Wyeth).

1969

11 July–8 September. First one-man museum show, *Oils, Watercolors and Drawings by James Wyeth,* Farnsworth Art Museum, Rockland, Maine.

Elected Associate of the National Academy of Design, one of youngest in institution's history.

Completes: *Portrait of Andrew Wyeth* (Collection of the Artist), *Apollo 11—One, Two, Three* (National Air and Space Museum, Smithsonian Institution), *Wide Load* (National Air and Space Museum, Smithsonian Institution), *Median Strip* (private collection).

1970

Completes: *Portrait of Pig* (Brandywine River Museum), *Sea of Storms* (private collection), *Gull Rock* (MBNA America).

1972

Appointed council member National Endowment for the Arts.

Completes: *Pumpkins at Sea* (private collection), *Newfoundland* (private collection) *Kent House*

(Brandywine River Museum), *The Red House* (Collection of the Artist), *Portrait of Jean Kennedy Smith* (private collection), *Pumpkinhead—Self Portrait* (private collection).

1973
Completes: *Portrait of Paul Mellon* (private collection—commissioned by sitter).

1974
James Wyeth Recent Paintings, first exhibition at Coe Kerr Gallery, New York City, which represents him until it closes, 1993.
Commissioned by *Harper's Magazine* to be court artist for Watergate trials. Sketches published throughout special issue, "American Character: Trial and Triumph," *Harper's Magazine* 249, no. 1493 (October 1974).
First meets Nureyev. Asks dancer to pose for portrait, Nureyev declines.
Completes: *Shark* (private collection), *Scavenger* (private collection), *Angus* (private collection), *Grackles and Angus* (private collection).

1975
Invited by the Soviet government's Union of Artists and Writers to visit U.S.S.R. art centers and speak to members.

Awarded honorary Doctor of Letters from Elizabethtown College, Elizabethtown, Pennsylvania.
Completes: *And Then Into the Deep Gorge* (private collection), *Portrait of Thomas Jefferson* (private collection), *The Islander* (Collection of Mr. and Mrs. Andrew Wyeth).

1976
Invited by Andy Warhol to paint in Warhol's Broadway studio known as "The Factory." The two artists paint portraits of each other. Exhibition, *Portraits of Each Other,* organized by Coe Kerr Gallery, New York City. Travels to Everson Museum of Art, Syracuse, New York; Tennessee Botanical Gardens and Fine Arts Center at Cheekwood, Nashville, Tennessee; Brandywine River Museum, Chadds Ford, Pennsylvania; and Hotel de Paris, Monaco.
Exhibition, *James Wyeth,* organized by Coe Kerr Gallery, New York City, travels to Joslyn Art Museum, Omaha, Nebraska. (Art Historian Theodore E. Stebbins, Jr., writes essay for exhibition catalogue.) *Portrait of Thomas Jefferson* appears in *Time* (July 4, Bicentennial issue).
Completed portrait of President-Elect Jimmy Carter published on cover of *Time* (January 1977), when Carter is named "Man of the Year." Associated pencil studies appear in *The New Republic,* 22 January 1977.
Completes: *Portrait of Andy Warhol* (Tennessee Fine Arts Center at Cheekwood), *Jimmy Carter* (National Portrait Gallery, gift of *Time), Man From Boston* (private collection).

1977

Meets Nureyev again. Dancer agrees to pose for portrait. Watches rehearsals from the wings at Uris Theater, New York City. Completes series of over thirty portrait studies and one large oil. Lincoln Kirstein purchases a study.

Completes: *Portrait of Rudolf Nureyev* (private collection), *Portrait of Arnold Schwarzenegger* (private collection—completed in "The Factory"), *Giant Clam* (private collection), *The Rookery* (Pepsico, Inc.).

1978

Completes: *Monhegan Bell* (MBNA America), *Runaway Pig* (private collection), *Looking South* (private collection), *Whale* (private collection).

1979

Illustrates children's book, *The Stray,* written by Betsy James Wyeth, based on life and people in Chadds Ford, Pennsylvania. Published by Farrar, Straus & Giroux.

Completes: *Angeload* (private collection), *Automaton* (Collection of Mr. and Mrs. Frank E. Fowler), *Wicker* (Collection of Mr. and Mrs. Andrew Wyeth), pen and ink drawings for *The Stray* (Collection of the Artist).

1980

First major retrospective, *Jamie Wyeth,* organized by the Pennsylvania Academy of the Fine Arts. Travels to Greenville County Museum of Art, South Carolina; and to Amon Carter Museum of Art, Fort Worth, Texas. Accompanying book published by Houghton Mifflin. Experiments with etching and lithography.

Completes: *Raven* (Brandywine River Museum), *A Very Small Dog* (MBNA America), series of etchings called *The Farm,* lithographs *To Sail Against the Wind* and *A Sea Pumpkin.*

1981

Commissioned by President and Mrs. Reagan to paint *Christmas Eve at the White House,* reproduced as White House Christmas card.

Completes: *10W30* (Collection of Mr. and Mrs. Andrew Wyeth), *30 Dozen* (private collection), *Leghorns* (private collection).

1982

Completes: *Coast Guard Anchor* (Farnsworth Art Museum), *A Couple of Chairs Sitting Around the Coast of Maine* (private collection), *Feeding Ledge* (private collection), *Mallard* (private collection), *Tide* (private collection), *Coast Guard Issue* (MBNA America), *Island Geese* (private collection).

1983
Awarded honorary Doctor of Letters from Dickinson School of Law, Dickinson College, Carlisle, Pennsylvania.
Exhibition of recent work, *Jamie Wyeth in Alaska*, organized by Coe Kerr Gallery, New York City. Travels to Anchorage Fine Arts Museum, Anchorage; University of Alaska Museum, Fairbanks; and Alaska State Museum, Juneau.
Completes: *The Summer in Maine* (Collection of Leslie S. Turchin), *Night Chickens* (private collection), *Chadds Ford Inn Pumpkin Carve* (private collection), *Fall Roses* (private collection).

1984
Second commission by the Reagans, *Christmas Morning at the White House*, reproduced as White House Christmas card.
Exhibition, *Jamie Wyeth: An American View*, organized by Portland Museum of Art, Portland, Maine. Travels to Columbia Museum, Columbia, South Carolina; and The Oklahoma Art Center, Oklahoma City.
Completes: *Breakfast at Sea* (private collection), *Wolfbane* (Brandywine River Museum), *Kleberg* (Terra Museum of American Art).

1985
Completes: *Sea Star* (Terra Museum of American Art), *New Year's Calling* (private collection).

1986
Exhibition, *An American Vision: Three Generations of Wyeth Art*, organized by the Brandywine River Museum, and includes works by Andrew and N. C. Wyeth. Exhibition travels over the next two years to Washington, D.C.; Dallas, Texas; Chicago, Illinois; as well as Italy, England, Japan, and Russia. (Lincoln Kirstein writes essay for exhibition catalogue published by Bullfinch Press.)
Completes: *Newt of Monhegan* (private collection), *Kalounna in Frogtown* (Terra Museum of American Art), *Southern Light* (private collection).

1987
Completes: *Scotia Prince* (private collection), *Connemara* (private collection), *Giuliana and the Sunflowers* (Brandywine River Museum), *The Influence Rose* (private collection).

1988
Awarded honorary doctoral degree from University of Vermont, Burlington.

Completes: *Gull's Egg* (Collection of the Artist), *Russians Off the Coast of Maine* (MBNA America), *Sable* (private collection), *Fog Bound Island* (private collection).

1989
Begins painting Monhegan Island teenager, Orca Bates, who figures prominently in his work of the early 1990s.

Completes: *Sesquicentennial* (Collection of Mr. Daniel K. Thorne), *Love the Giver* (private collection), *Door Wolf* (private collection), *Squirrelling* (Collection of the Artist), *Portrait of Orca Bates* (Farnsworth Art Museum).

1990
Jefferson (private collection), mixed media portrait of the president, on long-term loan at Monticello.
Moves to lightkeeper's house on Southern Island, off Tenants Harbor, Maine.

Completes: *Russian Circus Bear* (private collection), *Islanders* (private collection), *Orca Bates* (private collection), *Orca in Winter* (private collection).

1991
Completes: *Portrait of Richard Paul Mills* (private collection), *Buoy Tree* (private collection), *Connemara Four* (Cawley Family Collection).

1992
Completes: *Bi-Coastal* (private collection), *Michael, 21st Earl of Suffolk and the 14th Earl of Berkshire* (private collection), *The Mainland* (private collection), *The Wanderer* (private collection), *Light Station* (MBNA America).

1993
Exhibition, *Jamie Wyeth: Islands,* works completed on Maine islands, organized by the Farnsworth Art Museum.
6 January. Nureyev dies in Paris.
Three-Quarter Figure, Study for Portrait of Rudolf Nureyev, Study #91 (Collection of Albert, Kathlene, and Catharine Parnell) exhibited at Russian Embassy, Washington, D.C., during memorial service for Nureyev.
White Highlights, Three-Quarter Figure, Nureyev, Study # 15 (Collection of the Artist) exhibited in Ambassador's residence in Paris from 1993 to 1997.
Awarded honorary Doctor of Letters from Westbrook College, Portland, Maine.

Completes: *Lighthouse* (private collection), *Iris at Sea* (private collection), *Meteor Shower* (Collection of Mr. and Mrs. Andrew Wyeth), *Black Background, Three-Quarter Figure, Nureyev* (Collection of the Artist), *White Highlights, Three-Quarter Figure, Nureyev* (Collection of the Artist), *Nude, Three-Quarter Figure, Nureyev* (Collection of the Artist), *Yellow Leotard, Three-Quarter Figure, Nureyev* (private collection).

1994
Receives commission to create portrait of Eunice
Kennedy Shriver for 1995 Special Olympics World
Summer Games Commemorative Coin (May 1995,
Philadelphia Mint).
Completes: *Cat and Mouse* (private collection), *Screen
Door to the Sea* (Farnsworth Art Museum), *Black Spruce*
(Kemper Museum of Contemporary Art).

1995
Completes: *Cat Bates of Monhegan* (private collection),
Other Voices (private collection), *Dome Room* (Warner
Collection), *Sunset, Southern Island* (private collection).

1996
5 January. Lincoln Kirstein dies.
Completes: *Vice President's House* (private collection),
Nine is a Secret (private collection), *If Once You Have
Slept on an Island* (private collection), *The Thief* (MBNA
America), *Sophomore at Bowdoin* (private collection),
paintings for *Cabbages and Kings* (Collection of the Artist).

1997
Illustrates children's book, *Cabbages and Kings,*
published by Viking, text by Elizabeth Seabrook.
Exhibition, *N. C. Wyeth and his Grandson: A Legacy,*
organized by the Terra Museum of American Art,
Chicago, Illinois. Travels to Brandywine River
Museum, Chadds Ford, Pennsylvania.
Completes: *Saltwater Ice* (private collection), *Comet*
(MBNA America), *Wolfgang of Monhegan* (private
collection), *Lighthouse Dandelions* (MBNA America).

1998
Wyeth Center opens, Farnsworth Art Museum.
Includes gallery spaces, archive storage, and
research library. Inaugural exhibition, *Wondrous
Strange,* also features works by Howard Pyle and
N. C. and Andrew Wyeth. Exhibition travels
to Delaware Art Museum, Wilmington.
Completes: *Ice Storm, Maine* (private collection), *Katie
on Southern* (private collection), *Maine Coon Cat* (MBNA
America), *Harbor, Monhegan* (MBNA America).

1999
Exhibition, *Dead Cat Museum, Monhegan Island,* organized
by James Graham and Sons, New York City.
Completes: *Drink* (Collection of Mr. and Mrs. Andrew
Wyeth), *Eat* (Farnsworth Art Museum), *The Church*
(MBNA America), *The Wind* (private collection), *The
Tempest, a Triptych* (MBNA America), *Julia on the Swing*
(Cawley Family Collection), *Dead Cat Museum, Monhegan
Island* (Cawley Family Collection).

2000

Exhibition of political-theme paintings, *One Nation: Patriots and Pirates Portrayed by N. C. Wyeth and James Wyeth,* organized by the Farnsworth Art Museum. Travels to Russell Rotunda at the Capitol, Washington, D.C. (coincides with inauguration of George W. Bush, January 2001). Additional venues include: New Britain Museum of American Art, Connecticut; Brandywine River Museum, Chadds Ford, Pennsylvania; and Ringling Museum of Art, Sarasota, Florida.

Completes: *Dawn, The White House, 2000* (The White House Historical Association), *Fogbank* (MBNA America), *Hillgirt Farm* (Brandywine River Museum), *Final Approach Into Philadelphia* (MBNA America), *The Island's Schoolteacher* (Collection of Bebe and Crosby Kemper).

2001

Awarded honorary Doctor of Letters from the University of Maine, Orono.

Completes: *The Raven and the Girl* (private collection), *Iceberg* (private collection), *Portrait of Nureyev* (Collection of Jim and Jocelyn Stewart), *Nureyev—Purple Scarf* (Collection of the Artist), *Nureyev—Don Quixote— Yellow Background* (Collection of the Artist), *Nureyev— Don Quixote—White Background* (Collection of the Artist), *Nureyev—Swan Lake* (Collection of the Artist), *Mort de Noureev* (Collection of the Artist), *Curtain Call* (Collection of the Artist).

SELECTED BIBLIOGRAPHY

JAMES WYETH

Carpenter, Sandra, and Greg Schaber. "Jamie Wyeth: His Art and Insights." *The Artist's Magazine* (August 1997): 36–42.

Duff, James H., Andrew Wyeth, Thomas Hoving, Lincoln Kirstein. *An American Vision: Three Generations of Wyeth Art.* Boston: Bulfinch Press, 1987.

Heiser, Scott. "Down on the Farm with Jamie Wyeth." *Interview* (February 1974): 12–14.

"How Jamie Wyeth Paints People." In *Art and Man* 8, no. 5 (March 1978): 4–5.

Jamie Wyeth: An American View. Exhibition catalogue. Introduction by Michael Preble. Portland, Maine: Portland Museum of Art, 1984.

James Wyeth. Exhibition catalogue. Introduction by Professor Theodore E. Stebbins, Jr. New York: Coe Kerr Gallery, 1976.

James Wyeth Paintings. Exhibition catalogue. Introduction by Lincoln Kirstein. New York: M. Knoedler and Co., Inc., 1966.

Patton, Phil. "Painting's Favorite Son." *United Mainliner* (October 1980): 64–67, 112–15.

Stoner, Joyce Hill. *A Closer Look.* Wilmington: Delaware Art Museum, 1998.

Wetmore, Gordon. "Jamie Wyeth: Painter of Patriots, Presidents, Seagulls and the White House." *International Artist* 18 (April/May 2001): 44–53.

Wyeth, Jamie. *Jamie Wyeth.* Boston: Houghton Mifflin, 1980.

RUDOLF NUREYEV

Albert, Gennady. *Alexander Puskin: Master Teacher.* New York: The New York Public Library for the Performing Arts, 2001.

Barnes, Clive. *Nureyev.* New York: Helene Obolensky Enterprises, 1982.

Bland, Alexander. *Fonteyn and Nureyev: The Story of a Partnership.* London: Orbis, 1979; and New York: Times Books, 1979.

Bland, Alexander. *The Nureyev Image.* New York: Quadrangle/New York Times Books, 1976.

Brown, Howard, ed. and des. *Nureyev.* London: Phaidon Press, 1993.

Dantzig, Rudi van. *Noerejev: Het spoor can een komeet.* Zutphen: Gaipparde Pers, 1994.

Fonteyn, Margot. *Autobiography.* London: W. H. Allen, 1975; and New York: Alfred A. Knopf, 1976.

Nureyev, Rudolf. *Nureyev: An Autobiography with Pictures.* Edited by Alexander Bland. London: Hodder & Stoughton, 1962.

Pasi, Mario. *Nureyev: La sua arte, la sua vita.* Milano: Sperling & Kupfer, 1993.

Percival, John. *Nureyev: Aspects of the Dancer.* New York: Putnam, 1975; London and New York: Granada Publishing, 1979.

Péres, Louis. *Rudolf Nureyev.* Text by Arthur Todd. New York: Dance Horizons, 1975.

Solway, Diane. *Nureyev: His Life.* London: Weidenfeld & Nicolson, 1998; and New York: William Morrow, 1998.

Tracy, Robert. *Goddess: Martha Graham's Dancers Remember.* New York: Limelight Editions, 1997.

Watson, Peter. *Nureyev: A Biography.* London: Hodder & Stoughton, 1994.

Zakrzhevskaia, T. I., Miasnikova, L. P., and Storozhuk, A. G., comps. *Rudolf Nureyev: Three Years in the Kirov Theatre.* Translated by Kenneth MacInnes. St. Petersburg: Pushkinsky Foundation, 1995.

INDEX

NOTE: PAGE NUMBERS IN ITALICS REFERENCE ILLUSTRATIONS, ASTERISKS DENOTE WYETH WORKS NOT INCLUDED IN EXHIBITION.